THE MIND IS JUST LIKE A MUSCLE

ALSO BY SARA SALAM

If Water Were Fire, A Novel

If Love Were Salt, A Novel

My Truth Journal

Love Isn't Linear: A Collection of Poems About

Modern Love

My Newport: A Collection of Poems About

Newport Beach, California

Remember When: A Collection of Poems By A

Lovestruck Teen Who Had The Courage to Dream

THE MIND IS JUST LIKE A MUSCLE

A SELF-HELP BOOK FOR TEENS ON GROWING UP IN MODERN AMERICA

BY SARA SALAM

The Peacock Pen Press

2020

Copyright © 2020 Sara Salam

All rights reserved. No part of this book may be used in any manner whatsoever without written permission, except in the case of brief quotations and reviews.

ISBN: 978-1-953636-00-3 (Paperback)
ISBN: 978-1-953636-01-0 (Hardcover)
ISBN: 978-1-953636-02-7 (eBook)

Library of Congress Control Number: 2020916690
1. Teen- Young Adult
2. Self-Help
3. STEM
4. History
5. Diversity
6. Unconscious Bias

Book cover design by Aspen Denita.
Author portrait by Christina Wehbe.
Edited by Anna Alger.

Icons from the Noun Project:
Airplane by Egorova Valentina; Thinking by ProSymbols; Levitating brain by Dairy Free Design; House by Andi Nur Abdillah; Brain by Eucalyp ; Workout by Becris; Dishware by Olena Panasovska; Lightning by Martial Red; Earth by Serhii Smirnov; Brain Technology by Vectors Point; Ship by kareemovic2000; Bun by Flatart; Bubbles by Serhii Smirnov; Projector by Econceptive; Gender symbol by Anagaja Design; Heart by Alena Artemova; Helicopter by angga firdaus; Rosie the Riveter by Katunger; Hen by Vectors Point; Question Mark by Gabriele Malaspina; and Magnifying Glass by Elizabeth Lopez.

Printed by The Peacock Pen Press in the United States of America.

First Printing Edition 2020.

© 2020 Sara Salam

🌐 www.bysarasalam.com

📷 @bysarasalam

▶ Sara Salam

For all the brave teens just trying to figure it out.

CONTENTS

PREFACE	1
INTRODUCTION	3
PART I: THE HUMAN BRAIN	18
PART II: INSIDE & OUTSIDE THE HOUSEHOLD	51
PART III: TAKING ACTION WITH EXERCISE	85
CONCLUDING WORDS	92
THANK YOU!	I
ACKNOWLEDGMENTS	II
ABOUT THE AUTHOR	IV
APPENDIX: NOTES FROM MY BLOG	V
REFERENCES	XIV

PREFACE

At the time of this book's publication, the state of the world is one of unprecedented confusion and chaos. For context, I started researching and writing the content of this book in January of 2020.

How 2020 unfolded didn't change the scope of what I wanted to write, but it did illuminate, more than ever before, how living in such an interconnected world affects the ways we manage relationships, both on an individual level and on group levels (family, friends, classmates, co-workers, government, etc.). One could argue it's because of the world's interconnectedness that we are living in a state of crisis, across many dimensions, in the first place.

The key point is, there is so much unknown, which can be really scary. We are still learning how to best navigate through it all. We're building the plane while flying it, to a certain extent.

THE MIND IS JUST LIKE A MUSCLE

The goal of this book is to explore:

1. **Why** what we don't know scares us
2. **How** to overcome (or at least acknowledge and mitigate) these fears

The idea for this book was planted by a good friend who, upon reading one of my novels, suggested I write a self-help book to help young people feel less alone in navigating this complicated world. Here we are, twenty thousand-plus words later.

At the end of the day, information is our greatest armor. Granted, too much information and the *wrong* information can be devastating, so we need to be mindful of our sources and how we apply the knowledge we gain. It's about collecting and analyzing the data, and using our brains to make the most educated choices about how to solve the problem at hand. We need to use our tools responsibly, so they don't inadvertently become weapons.

INTRODUCTION

EVERYONE IS GOING THROUGH IT

We live in a torrential time. Everyone is confused, overwhelmed, and/or stressed—more often than not, some combination of the three. The speed at which the world is changing is unlike any other time in the history of humankind.

There are the things that are intangible, yet visible to the naked eye. We're living in the midst of an infotech and biotech revolution, complete with an alphabet soup of AI, AR, VR, machine learning, blockchain, cryptocurrency. All these developments are products about twenty years (give or take) in the making.

There are the things we see plain as day in the news and in our neighborhoods. We're living in a time where much is visible and reaches our brain almost as quickly as they happen.

THE MIND IS JUST LIKE A MUSCLE

PRETTY "BIG" U.S. EVENTS IN 2020 (THROUGH AUGUST)

NBA Legend Kobe Bryant is killed

COVID-19 reaches global pandemic levels, affecting many dimensions of life including but not limited to economics and public health (this could be a whole section, really)

President Donald Trump Impeached and Acquitted

The federal case centered around Jeffrey Epstein grows

Protests and demonstrations centered around Black Lives Matter grow

SpaceX launches Falcon 9 from NASA's Kennedy Space Center

Kamala Harris becomes first Indian American and woman of color on a major party ticket as Joe Biden's VP nominee for the Democratic Party

Why do we feel so stressed out?

Quite simply, our brains are having trouble keeping up with all the excitement. The capacity of our biology, i.e. our brains, is not equipped to evolve quickly enough to keep pace with these changes.

Does that sound like nonsense? Take a look at this graph, which illustrates the relationship between the year (x-axis) and the world population (y-axis). It maps the evolution of the brain alongside the technology advancements of the world since the first agricultural revolution.

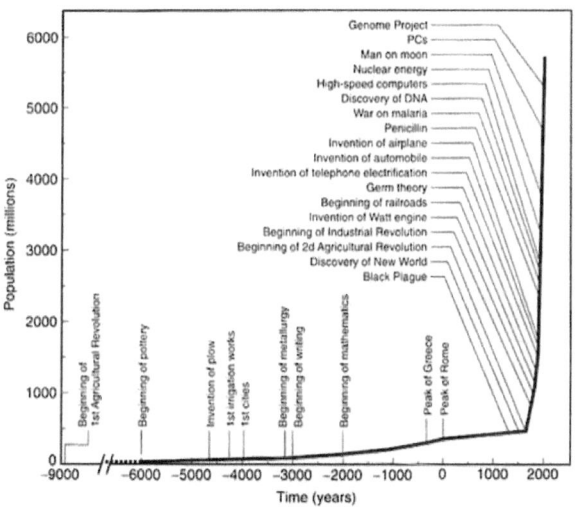

This graph is by no means all-inclusive. It captures critical achievements in the history of human invention and shows how the pace of human invention has recently sped up ("recently" is a relative term, as we'll see). The rate at which the brain evolves, though, has not.

The neocortex, for example, is a new-ish part of the brain that has evolved within the last 20,000 years. Compared with the existence of modern man, or homo sapiens, which dates back about 2.5 million years, this is a relatively recent development.

The takeaway: if history is any indication, the pace of our brain evolution is not prepared to keep up with the pace of technological advancement. There is a serious lag, and it's showing up in how we experience the

THE MIND IS JUST LIKE A MUSCLE

world; notably in various forms of stress, including violence, exhaustion, disease, and other debilitating consequences.

The lesson: as our biology evolves—often in response to the world we live in—so do our brains. Today, the pace of evolution just isn't as fast as modern technology.

Sometimes we forget the brain behaves a lot like a muscle.

> Sometimes we forget the brain behaves a lot like a muscle.

(According to the most up-to-date research, the brain is not anatomically a muscle. It's actually made of 60% fat! In fact, it is the mind—the product of our brain activity, or our cognitive ability—that acts like a muscle. Distinguishing between the brain and the mind is the subject of another book entirely, so to make things more straightforward, in this text we'll treat the brain and the mind as two parts of the same whole.)

Why does this matter? Because muscles need exercise to get bigger and stronger. Just like your biceps or quads, the brain needs "workouts" to grow . For the biceps, this could be dumbbell curls or push-ups. For the brain, it could be reading a news article or solving a puzzle. The more we exercise our brains, the stronger they get. We'll learn more about the science of the brain in Part I.

How has modern technology affected our brains? Take, for example, the number of interactions we have per day. People are met with 11 million bits of stimuli at any given moment, and face 35,000 decisions per day.. How overwhelming is that?

And it is overwhelming for everyone, whether we realize it or not. You're not alone.

This book explores both nature and nurture—how we're built as humans, and the consequent effects of our environment on our behavior. We'll discover the nuances of the experiences that make us human, and how that translates into how we experience modern America.

HOW ELSE IS OUR WORLD DIFFERENT?

In a word: people. In our increasingly globalized, technology-impacted, shrinking world, we encounter a more diverse range of individuals, not to mention growing numbers of people. Recall the previous graph, where the y-axis represents population growth.

Did you know our grandparents saw as many people in one month as we do in one day? What's more, in the early days of humans millions of years ago, people only saw their "clan-mates" on a daily basis. Sometimes they encountered other nomadic tribes when moving from one locale to another in search of food, but it could be days or weeks before these meetings took place.

Today, we live in a world where transportation and accessibility has changed not only the means and how often we communicate with each other, but how we engage and physically exist with each other. In the United States in particular, immigrants, multicultural individuals, and refugees make up a significant portion of the population. We'll get into more detail on what this means for living in modern America later.

The focus of this book is to build awareness around how interconnectedness can affect us on an individual level, and how these effects can in turn create a different set of challenges for society at large.

> The focus of this book is to build awareness around how interconnectedness can affect us on an individual level, and how these effects can in turn create a different set of challenges for society at large.

SARA SALAM

WHY THIS BOOK?

As the product of a multicultural household, I grew up in a time when the term "multiculturalism" wasn't such a common word in one's vocabulary—though, as we've just noted, the concept has been around since the first groups of humans interacted with other groups of humans. My name, for example, is both biblical and quranic. The Bible and Qur'an are the top two best-selling books in the history of the world.

I was one of few kids in my hometown that grew up in a "hybrid home", which presented its own challenges when it came to my identity. I considered focusing the content of this book for an audience that had similar shared experiences based on cultural differences, and how that played out while growing up.

I decided against that for one really, really good reason.

Based on my extensive research into history, psychology, sociology, economics, politics, and math, I have found that all humans have a shared biological makeup (sounds obvious, right?). Yet—and this is key—how our humanness is expressed varies based on numerous factors. While growing up in a multicultural household definitely has its nuances, there are other variables not necessarily correlated with culture that affect how we see the world. These themes are addressed in this book.

While not exhaustive, the goal of this book is to encourage awareness around these variables, and how they might play a role in shaping how you think of yourself, and how you think about and engage with the world at large.

THE MIND IS JUST LIKE A MUSCLE

It's important to be aware of these variables, these realities, and to accept them, so when it's time to enter the real world you are armed with the tools and insights that will help you be a successful, empathetic citizen.

> It's important to be aware of these variables, these realities, and to accept them, so when it's time to enter the real world you are armed with the tools and insights that will help you be successful, empathetic citizens.

WHAT TO EXPECT

In Part I, we first dig into the human form and function—specifically the brain, and how it affects our experience of the world. We'll look at different sections of the brain, their various functions, and how they influence our behavior[1].

---

[1] For our purposes, we'll focus on a high level overview. We won't get into specifics around the effects of development, disease, and other factors. We'll save that for another book.

Then, with these behaviors as our standard of reference, we identify human-made concepts that illustrate these behaviors. For you history buffs, these will include ideas such as ethnocentrism, groupthink, and unconscious bias. We'll go through some historical and modern examples so we understand how these science-y concepts actually play out in real life.

In Part II, we'll zero in on the household itself, focusing on what happens both inside and outside the home, so we can build as complete a picture as possible of reality. We'll look in detail at core themes, including familial relationships and the role of media and politics.

Part III summarizes key takeaways and actionable lessons you can apply to your life and how you navigate it. We all have different experiences, and taking into account your goals and the tools you have, we hope that puts you in an infinitely better position to succeed, whatever that means for you.

WHO ARE YOU?

Over the last few years there has been a surge in interest around family lineage, made digitally discoverable by 23andMe, Ancestry, and other such genomic platforms. As of January 2019, over 26 million people had taken an ancestry test. It reflects a curiosity in many about learning of their families, their pasts, and their identities. The desire to learn is a good thing! You'll see why when we get to Part II. Craving knowledge about ourselves and educating ourselves and each other is the key to empowerment, for ourselves and for each other.

THE MIND IS JUST LIKE A MUSCLE

The reality is, an overwhelming majority of Americans are descendants of immigrants. (The exception are indigenous tribes.) As explained by the Oxford Dictionary, an immigrant is a person who comes to live permanently in a foreign country. America's Founding Fathers, hailing from England, are immigrants by definition. Therefore, their posterity are descendants of immigrants.

Whether we choose to identify ourselves as such often dictates our point of view.

Prejudice is rooted in perspective, often a direct result of limited information. Why? Because, and this is important: **What we don't know scares us**. This is why education is so important; it's crucial to bring light to the shadows, to build awareness and encourage acceptance.

Think about it this way: Why is the darkness so scary? Because it's unknown, mysterious, unfamiliar. Because we don't have the knowledge or the information to explain it.

What we don't know scares us.

> **WHAT WE DON'T KNOW SCARES US.**

When you walk into a room and you don't know anyone, you may feel a sensation of dread, fear, or discomfort. Some people thrive on the unknown, and make no mistake—this is a learned trait. It can be taught.

Why do we feel these feelings?

Because what we don't know scares us. The unfamiliar is programmed in our brains as something to fear. You know the saying, "Knowledge is power"? The best way to overcome fear is to educate and train ourselves to develop informed awareness around the situation, accept the reality, and respond accordingly.

How do we react? Our brains engage in one of three responses: fight, flight, or freeze. We'll explore each response in greater detail in Part I.

What does this mean for those of us who are "different"? We are treated as unknown, mysterious, and unfamiliar, and therefore are reacted to by others with either fight, flight, or freeze responses.

Spoiler alert: We are all different. We bond over similarities because they make us feel safe. We worry about differences because they make us feel afraid. How do we overcome this? By learning about each other and identifying/noticing what's shared.

ASSUMPTIONS

Because I am a human writing this book, I have my own lens through which I am sharing my insights. While the purpose of this book is not to recount all of the things that make me, *me* (though I am committed

THE MIND IS JUST LIKE A MUSCLE

to writing an autobiography one day), I think it is important to outline a few key assumptions which inform my outlook on this subject matter.

1. All experiences occur on a continuum. In fact, many of our human-made systems and explanations for outcomes or ways of being are binary, or a duality. A duality is an instance of opposition or contrast between two concepts or two aspects of something. I describe it as two poles on opposite ends of a spectrum. Most human disposition occurs on a spectrum: happiness/sadness, hope/fear, nature/nurture, even introversion/extroversion. Each of these are pairs of opposites, where the space between is a spectrum representative of moderate forms of these behaviors—the poles being the extremes.

The image below, for example, illustrates the spectrum of extroversion, showing the range of possibilities between the two extremes (introvert and extrovert) including the moderate "ambivert."

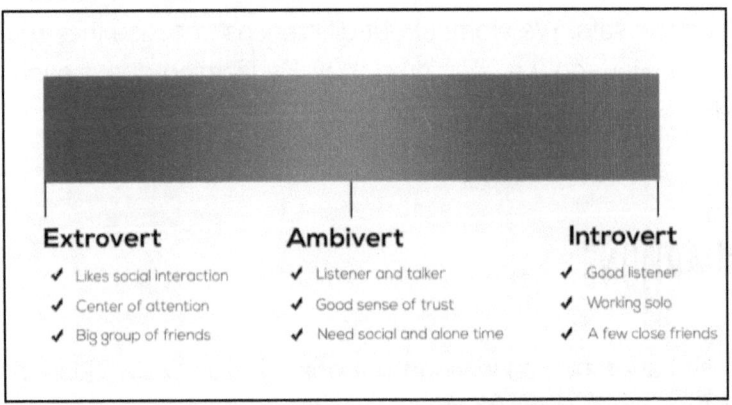

In short, these constructs help us explain and categorize the world. We'll learn more about how and why in Part 1.

Which brings us to the second assumption:

2. There are always going to be clusters of people on a continuum, where more people will fall than others. If you like math, you might think of it as (perhaps an ironically named) "normal" distribution.

In the graph below, the top of the curve represents the highest occurrence of whatever variable is being measured—the average. Think of test scores, for example. When you plot the scores of a class on a graph, a lot of the time you will see a cluster, which represents the average score.

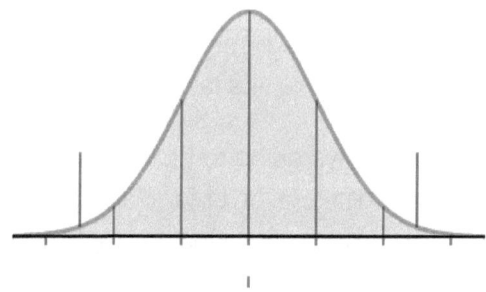

The implication of this book's concept is, the information I share is from these clusters, mainly because the information available in research limits me to this data set. It's part of research methodology that predates modern science. (It's one of the ironies of education: There's always something new to discover, which is why research is so important.)

Which brings me to the third and perhaps most important assumption:

THE MIND IS JUST LIKE A MUSCLE

3. Everyone is different. There are many people that lie outside of the clusters, the average, the typical, the majority. The majority can often be what is most familiar or most publicized because of sheer volume, and thus relatability across the masses. The reality is, the baseline for normal is changing constantly as we become more aware of each other, and as we educate ourselves. It's also possible for people to fall outside of a continuum, or duality/binary construct.

Consider the concept of gender, which has taken on a more fluid dynamic in modern discourse. Most of us are familiar with the male, female, and transgender labels. The muxe gender, in addition, is a respected third gender in Zapotec cultures in Oaxaca, Mexico that has existed for centuries. In fact, there are other notions of a third gender acknowledged by other cultures across the globe as well. In some Native American cultures, the umbrella term to describe a third gender is "two-spirit." In South Asia, it's hijras. In Thailand, it's kathoeys. In Ethiopia, it's ashtime. In Polynesia, it's fa'afafine.

Suffice it to say, there's always going to be a person, concept or idea that you might consider different or unfamiliar. The choice you can make is to be aware of it and acknowledge the implications for yourself, if any.

And so, keep in mind that the ideas presented in this book are in fact rooted in research, but that doesn't mean that they represent every person's reality. There's simply no such thing.

Then why write this book? Because that's exactly the point: to acknowledge that differences exist, and to foster conversations around why that is and how these differences affect our realities and perceptions of reality.

SARA SALAM

My motto is: Truth is personal. Using the information, knowledge, and resources we have, let's take a look at why we are the way we are, how that can play out in our lives, and the roles we can play to shape them.

PART I: THE HUMAN BRAIN

What makes the human brain different from other mammal brains? Humans possess consciousness, a concept that has been and is still being researched and debated among scientists and philosophers alike. For our purposes, we'll define consciousness as self-awareness—the ability to make perceptions about the self and the relationship of the self to the world. This unique trait gives us the ability to tell stories. We use stories to make meaning of the world—which, as far as we know today, other animals are unable to do. (Maybe they do, and we just don't know it yet. Jury's still out.) We'll explore how storytelling affects how we interact with each other and the world later.

In this section, we'll explore the human brain and dig into some of the key parts and functions that affect how we think, feel, and interact with each other. This includes the greater nervous system, the brain itself, and the many components that work together to ensure our bodies work in harmony.

First, a bit about the brain.

OVERVIEW: THE BRAIN AND THE NERVOUS SYSTEM

The human brain is basically a powerful central server that stores our memory and controls how we think, react, and interact. Even today, there are still features and functions that scientists continue to explore and research due to the brain's complexity.

The brain is the center of the human nervous system, responsible for controlling our thoughts, movements, memories, and decisions. Even accounting for the relatively slow pace of evolution, the human brain has become more and more complicated.

The nervous system is made up of around 100 billion nerve cells, called neurons, which are microscopic cells. They get the messages from your senses, including seeing, hearing, tasting, smelling, touching, and moving.

> Fun fact: You can still make new connections even when you are 100 years old. Your older relatives may not learn how to code or upload content as fast as you, but they are more than capable!

When you learn things, the messages travel from one neuron to another, again and again, creating pathways so things become easier for you and you get better at them over time.

There are over one trillion neurons in your brain. Your brain collects all the information, sorts it out, thinks, remembers, creates, compares, solves problems, and coordinates actions all at the same time, even while you're sleeping.

Your brain keeps on growing until you are about twenty years old. By that time, the brain has made plenty of connections which it no longer needs, and therefore removes any unnecessary connections. It still has billions of brain cells left to help you through the rest of your life. Fun fact: You can still make new connections even when you are 100 years old. Your older relatives may not learn how to code or upload content as fast as you, but they are more than capable!

MAIN PARTS OF THE BRAIN

Your brain has three main parts: the cerebrum, the cerebellum, and the brain stem. The part of the brain that impacts how we make choices and interact with our environments (people, places, things, ideas) is the cerebrum, which also happens to make up about two-thirds of the total mass of the brain.

THE CEREBRUM

The cerebrum is the largest and widest region of the brain. A longitudinal deep groove known as the longitudinal fissure divides the cerebrum into two equal, symmetrical halves; the left and right hemispheres. One of the ironies of the brain: The left side of the brain controls the right side of the body, and the right side of the brain controls the left side of the body.

Each cerebral hemisphere is further divided into four lobes; the frontal lobe, the parietal lobe, the temporal lobe, and the occipital lobe.

The outer extensively folded region of the cerebrum is called the cerebral cortex, which consists of grey matter. The grey matter is made up of what are called cortical layers: the neocortex and the allocortex.The neocortex consists of six layers of neurons, while the allocortex is made up of three to four layers of neurons.

THE NEOCORTEX

As we learned earlier, the neocortex is a new-ish part of the brain, having evolved in humans within the last 20,000 years. The neocortex increased in size in response to pressures for greater cooperation and competition in early ancestors. With the size increase, there was greater voluntary inhibitory control of social behaviors, resulting in increased social harmony. (Foresight: it will be interesting to see how our brains evolve with the onset of modern living and all that entails.)

THE PREFRONTAL CORTEX

The prefrontal cortex is the cerebral cortex covering the front part of the frontal lobe. The brain of a teenager does not have a completely developed prefrontal cortex. The prefrontal cortex is the brain region associated with the functions of decision making, complex thinking behavior, expression of the personality, and social behavior. That is why teenagers are so emotional, often show dangerous behaviors, and take risks. Because this part of the brain is not fully developed yet, it is more reactive. It's similar to why babies cry all the time; they haven't developed their capacity for language yet. It all comes back to the brain.

THE AMYGDALA

Your brain has a cluster of cells on each side called the amygdala. The word amygdala is Latin for almond, and that's what this area looks like. Scientists believe that the amygdala is responsible for emotion. It's normal to feel all different kinds of emotions, good and bad. Sometimes you might feel a little sad, and other times you might feel scared, or silly, or glad. Essentially, the amygdala's job is to figure out what parts of the environment are threatening and remind us to stay away from them, and what parts are welcoming and meant to be enjoyed.

The amygdala is involved in learning and, specifically, a type of learning called fear conditioning—tracking what kinds of things predict bad outcomes.

For example, if I see a mountain lion while I'm out walking my dog, I will experience fear—in the form of a quickly beating heart, sweaty palms, and deeper than normal breaths. This response occurs because the millions of neurons in my brain process the situation and quickly calculate that the probability of serious injury—and if I'm really unfortunate, death—is high.

The same process takes place when I see a handsome man across the room. Feelings of attraction—in the form of a quickly beating heart, sweaty palms, and deeper than normal breaths—will occur if the chemical reactions in my brain calculate that this individual offers good mating or social bonding potential.

These biochemical formulas as they exist today were refined and developed over millions of years of evolution. If one of our ancestors was wrong and made a big, fatal mistake, the genes that led to that outcome did not pass on.

These feelings, reactions, and behaviors are all products of human biology: biochemical mechanisms that our brains and bodies use to increase the likelihood of survival and reproduction. Without these tools to help us survive and thrive, our species would die out and we would not exist. What's the point of that? And so, our brains are thus deeply complex yet imperfect tools that help us navigate and survive in the world.

IMPLICATIONS FOR BIAS

While somewhat puny in size, the amygdala has a drastic effect on human behavior, including and especially when it comes to expressions of bias—like prejudice, racism, and stereotypes.

As we learned, feelings are an expression of our brains' chemical reactions. These chemical reactions take place with the goal of ensuring survival and making sure our species continues to live on. This is an important point to remember.

Recall the environment that existed when humans first inhabited the earth: minimal encounters with people outside their tribe.

Bias is another form of fear conditioning. Recall that fear conditioning is a type of learning that tracks what kinds of things predict bad outcomes. As a result of the environment our ancestors inhabited, they basically learned to fear people who didn't look like them, people they didn't have personal relationships with, people who were strangers. Their brains were inherently biased against people they didn't know as a form of protection, of self-preservation. And so, millions of years later, because of the chemical reactions taking place in our brains intended

TEEN BRAIN RESEARCH

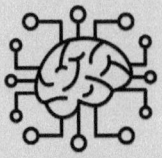

One study yielded some interesting findings as it relates to the teen brain's development and potential implications for mental health.

Basically, new brain networks activate during adolescence, allowing teenagers to develop more complex adult social skills. However, these new activations also increase the opportunity for the onset of mental illness. Why?

In short, the teenage brain wires and rewires itself much more frequently than the adult brain, increasing the possibility that, at some point along the road of development, the neurons in the teen brain might misfire and lead to complications.

The research team discovered that the way different regions of the brain communicate with each other changes in two main ways during adolescence. They have to do with connections between neurons in the brain getting stronger or becoming weaker as the brain ages into adulthood.

The brain regions that are important for vision, movement, and other basic faculties were strongly connected at the age of 14, and became even more strongly connected by the age of 25. However, the brain regions that are important for more advanced social skills, such as being able to imagine how someone else is thinking or feeling, showed a very different pattern of change: Areas that were poor in their connections became richer, and areas that were rich became poorer.

Based on these observations, it seems that "the acquisition of new, adult skills during adolescence depends on the active, disruptive formation of new connections between brain regions, bringing new brain networks 'online' for the first time to deliver advanced social and other skills as people grow older."

As one researcher noted: "We know that depression, anxiety and other mental health disorders often occur for the first time in adolescence-but we don't know why. These results show us that active re-modelling of brain networks is ongoing during the teenage years and deeper understanding of brain development could lead to deeper understanding of the causes of mental illness in young people."

As the teen brain is studied more, science will help us understand where along the road of development such disorders occur. Hopefully, this will give us an opportunity to address them early on and (ideally) mitigate them altogether.

to make sure our species continues, we still feel the effects—even though our world looks completely different. (Remember, the human brain evolves *very* slowly.)

In our increasingly connected world, we encounter new people every day. And yet, our brains are still naturally programmed to fight/flight/freeze.

How do we teach ourselves to not succumb to the way our brains have evolved to program our behaviors? Teaser: by building awareness and practicing acceptance.

One of the other cool things about being human is our ability to make conscious choices. It's through this consciousness that we are able to create stories (and one of the reasons you are able to enjoy this content today).

Despite the wiring of our brains, we can acknowledge the current world we live in and make decisions that are consistent with our beliefs as people, as a society. These beliefs will also vary from family to family, group to group, nation to nation. The key is in recognizing these differences exist and accepting these differences.

A TIMELY STUDY

In 2019, a study found people are hard-wired to process (or not process) facial differences based on race. And, perhaps most notably, that process occurs in the earliest filters of our thought process: our visual intake.

The consequences of noticing the differences in members of one own's race but not others have incredible implications, especially for affecting beliefs and behaviors. Such implications can range from an "oops" to potentially life-changing consequences.

"Members of minority groups wind up being exposed to more members of majority groups than majority members get exposed to minority members," said one researcher. "It could be that exposure to individuals of different groups may help the visual system develop expertise that reduces this effect."

Translation: being in a diverse environment and/or opening oneself up to different people (and learning about them) could help us be not so biased over time.

Perhaps most importantly, these effects are not uncontrollable. These biases in perception are malleable and subject to individual motivations and goals. Simply put, if we consciously make the effort to embrace people that are different from us, i.e. exercise our brains, the rate of prejudice and bias goes down.

Remember, prejudice is rooted in limited points of view, a one-dimensional perspective. This is why education is so important. Education brings light to the shadows—shadows of unknowns that create fear and foster hate. What we don't know scares us.

Let's explore some concepts that can help us understand how prejudice, bias, and stereotypes play out in how we think and how we organize ourselves. These concepts were created by scientists, philosophers, and psychologists—academics who have conducted research and made observations based on what they believe to be conclusive evidence.

We'll also look at some historical and modern examples of these concepts, so you can see how they play out in real life.

ETHNOCENTRISM

The Oxford English Dictionary defines ethnocentrism as the evaluation of other cultures according to preconceptions originating in the standards and customs of one's own culture. It was first applied in the social sciences by American sociologist William G. Sumner. In his 1906 book, *Folkways*, Sumner describes ethnocentrism as, "the technical name for the view of things in which one's own group is the center of everything, and all others are scaled and rated with reference to it." He further characterized ethnocentrism as often leading to pride, vanity, the belief in one's own group's superiority, and contempt for outsiders.

In summary, it's the use of one's own culture as the standard to judge other cultures. It's the assumption that one's own culture is the natural order of things and the "correct" way to live, the center of everything.

The irony is, most people tend to believe their culture is the center of the world, whether they're aware of it or not. Many Greeks believe history began with Homer, Sophocles, and Plato. Chinese nationalists believe history began with the Yellow Emperor and the Xia/Shang dynasties. The Hindus believe airplanes and bombs were invented by ancient Indian sages. Aztecs believed the sun would not rise and the universe would disintegrate if they didn't perform their ritual sacrifices every year; they literally believed the world revolved around them.

Why is ethnocentrism a form of bias? Because it could lead to false assumptions about cultural differences.

For example, an American might think that spoons, forks, and knives are the best way to eat. Whereas someone from a country like Japan or China might believe chopsticks are the best and correct way to consume a meal. Still other societies might favor the use of their hands.

In truth, none of these options is objectively the best or correct. Each is a preference, or a practice, rather than something that is absolute.

Another way to look at it can be found in historical examples of colonization, where one country seeks to "improve" the societies they colonize. Often, colonization would involve a ranking system based on the colonized peoples' adoption of ways of doing things and their achievement of significant milestones, such as religious conversion and technological advancement.

The barbarians, the gypsies, and the outcasts of society throughout history were the groups most often subjected to this ethnocentric approach to living. Examples include the British in India, Belgians in the Congo, China and Taiwan, Americans and Native Americans—the list goes on and on.

Anthropologist Francis Boas coined a term called cultural relativism, which removes the idea of inferiority and takes a more egalitarian approach to understanding differences across cultures. This is a great example of how over time, as we educate ourselves about each other and our preferences and practices, we become more aware and understanding. This puts us in a better position to accept our differences, rather than fear them.

Consider how we learn about history. When I was in school, we didn't learn about cultures outside the United States until sixth grade—and even then, it was about ancient civilizations, like Mesopotamia, Egypt,

THE MIND IS JUST LIKE A MUSCLE

Greece, etc. I didn't learn anything remotely detailed about current world affairs (in school) until tenth grade in AP World History. How is it even possible to cram all of the world's history into eight months of study? The answer is simple: it's not. The United States is not alone in prioritizing its country's history in school curriculums, and it makes sense for us to learn and understand the foundational truths upon which our country is built. However, it would behoove us to prioritize learning about the world earlier and more often throughout our primary and secondary schooling years—especially when it comes to understanding cultural diversity, arguably a constitutional truth of our country as well.

In kindergarten, we learned Christopher Columbus "discovered America" in 1492. But we didn't learn that Zheng He, an admiral from Ming dynasty China, landed in what is currently North America in 1421—about 70 years before Columbus. (Please note there is controversy around this point as well, as the notion was first introduced in 2002 by Gavin Menzies' book titled *1421*.)

We also learned that Johannes Gutenberg invented the printing press in 1453. But we didn't learn that in 1050, the Chinese used ceramics to create movable type themselves—a full three centuries prior to Gutenberg.

From what I understand, many school curriculums are being tweaked to account for our increasingly interconnected world and thus the knowledge we have about the world. The more aware we are of our world and what shapes it, the greater opportunity we have to shape it ourselves and make it better as best we can.

RELATED: XENOPHOBIA

Xenophobia is the fear or hatred of foreigners, people from different cultures, or strangers. There are several constructs that have grown out of this idea, including orientalism (which we touch on in the next section.)

Xenophobia is an expression of ethnocentrism, one of the consequences that can occur when a person or group of people believe and behave as though they are the center of the world, and it's "their way or the highway."

Again, history is ripe with examples. I've cited a few here, some that are common knowledge and others maybe not as well known. (If you search "xenophobia around the world" you will find tons more.) The key point is: prejudice and racism are not unique to one culture, as these behaviors are shared characteristics across human beings.

Ancient Romans, for instance, held notions of superiority over all other peoples. In a speech attributed to Manius Acilius, he proclaims:

"There, as you know, there were Macedonians and Thracians and Illyrians, all most warlike nations, here Syrians and Asiatic Greeks, the most **worthless** peoples among mankind and born for slavery."

Brazil

While the majority of the country's population is of mixed (also known as pardo), African, or indigenous descent, the presence of non-European Brazillians on the programming of most national television networks is scarce; in fact, it's typically limited to musicians and their shows. In telenovelas, Brazilians with darker skin tones are more often depicted as housekeepers or in positions of lower socioeconomic standing.

Canada

A 2016 survey from The Environics Institute found that there may be discriminating attitudes that may be a result of the effects of the September 11, 2001 attacks in the United States. Muslim and Sikh Canadians have faced racism and discrimination in recent years, especially since 2001.

Mexico

Historically, Mexicans with light skin tones had control over those with darker skin as a result of the structure of the Spanish colonial caste system. When a Mexican of a darker skin tone marries one of a lighter skin tone, it is common for them to say that they are "making the race better", or *"mejorando la raza"*. Despite improving economic and social conditions of Indigenous Mexicans, discrimination against Indigenous Mexicans continues, as there are few laws to protect them from discrimination.

Japan

Many reports have documented racism in Japan. In 2005, for example, a United Nations report by Doudou Diène (Special Rapporteur of the UN Commission on Human Rights) concluded that racial discrimination and xenophobia in Japan primarily affected three groups: national minorities, Latin Americans of Japanese descent (mainly Japanese Brazilians), and foreigners from poor countries. Surveys conducted in 2017 and 2019 have shown that 40 to nearly 50% of foreigners surveyed have experienced some form of discrimination.

Europe (as a whole)

A study that ran from 2002 to 2015 has mapped the countries in Europe with the highest incidents of racial bias towards black people, based on data from 288,076 white Europeans. Using the implicit-association test (a reaction-based psychological test designed to measure implicit racial bias), the strongest bias was found in several Eastern European countries—the Czech Republic, Lithuania, Belarus, Ukraine, Moldova, Bulgaria, and Slovakia—as well as Malta, Italy, and Portugal. A 2017 report by the University of Oslo Center for Research on Extremism tentatively suggested that "individuals of Muslim background stand out among perpetrators of antisemitic violence in Western Europe".

Uganda

Many individuals of South Asian descent inhabit what were once British colonies in sub-Saharan Africa. Brought by the British Empire from British India to do clerical work in imperial service, the most well-known case of anti-Indian racism was the ethnic cleansing of the Indian minority in Uganda by the dictator Idi Amin.

United States

I would be remiss not to acknowledge the xenophobia that exists in the history of the United States. This topic (as well as those cited above) are theses in many other books. The purpose here is to provide context for our central thesis: What we don't know scares us.

Xenophobia has existed since the colonial era, when white Americans were assigned legally or socially sanctioned privileges and rights, while the very same rights were denied to other races and minorities. For example, European Americans—particularly affluent, white Anglo-

Saxon Protestants—enjoyed exclusive privileges in matters of education, immigration, voting rights, citizenship, land acquisition, and criminal procedure throughout American history. Non-Protestant immigrants from Europe, particularly the Irish, Poles, and Italians, often suffered xenophobic exclusion and other forms of ethnicity-based discrimination in American society until the late 19th and early 20th centuries.

In addition, groups like Jews and Arabs have faced continuous discrimination in the United States, and as a result, some people who belong to these groups are not identified as white. African Americans have faced restrictions on their political, social, and economic freedom throughout much of US history. East, South, and Southeast Asians have similarly faced racism in America. Major racially and ethnically structured institutions include slavery, segregation, Native American reservations, Native American boarding schools, immigration and naturalization laws, and internment camps.

Formal racial discrimination was largely banned by the mid-20th century, and over time, it has come to be perceived as being socially and morally unacceptable. Racial politics remains a major phenomenon, and racism continues to be reflected in socioeconomic inequality. As current studies and research indicate, racial stratification continues to occur in employment, housing, education, lending, and government.

RELATED: ORIENTALISM

Another example of ethnocentrism (and by extension, xenophobia) as a philosophy in itself is orientalism. *Orientalism* is also a book by Edward W. Said published in 1978, where Said explains the idea of "Orientalism" to describe the West's historically snobbish representations of "The East," which in most scholarship tends to include people or groups that live in of Asia, North Africa, and the Middle East.

Said argued that Orientalism, in the sense of the Western scholarship about the Eastern World, is solely tied to the imperialist societies who produced it, which makes much Orientalist work inherently political and servile to power. These cultural representations refer in most cases to the "orient" as primitive, irrational, violent, despotic, fanatic—and essentially inferior to the westerner.

A key theme to note: We see a lot of examples of binaries throughout history and in our modern world, such as Democrats/ Republicans, introverts/ extroverts, cat people/ dog people. These dualities demonstrate the habit of people simplifying their worlds using "opposites." Another example: the yin and yang, which means that the universe is governed by a cosmic duality—sets of two opposing and complementing principles or cosmic energies that can be observed in nature.

In short, these constructs help us explain and categorize the world—again, a product of the brain's evolutionary priority to protect the species and ensure its survival. Categorizing makes it easier for our brains to identify whether something is safe or threatening, and that oversimplification extends to our modern challenges; though the landscape is very different and more complex as compared to early human society.

RELATED (KIND OF): COLOR BLINDNESS

I'm including color blindness because the underlying message is consistent with our theme of relativism. It also shows how perception affects many different dimensions of our lives.

If you have color blindness, it means you see colors differently than most people. Most of the time, color blindness makes it hard to tell the difference between certain colors.

Usually, color blindness runs in families. There's no cure. Most people who are color blind are able to adjust and don't have problems with everyday activities.

What's interesting is, color blindness by definition means seeing colors differently. The term "blindness" in this sense is a bit of a misnomer. Symptoms of color blindness are often so mild that you may not notice them. And since we get used to the way we see colors, many people with color blindness don't know they have it.

Everyone sees color a little differently—even people who aren't color blind. About 1 in 12 men are color blind. Most people with color blindness are born with it, but sometimes it doesn't show up until later in life. One of my family members is colorblind; he found out during a science class in eighth grade. Would he have been aware of the difference in how he perceives colors unless it had been pointed out to him? Maybe, maybe not.

The key point is: just because someone (literally) sees something differently doesn't make it wrong or incorrect. Sometimes it's circumstantial, sometimes it's a matter of preference, like chopsticks versus cutlery.

GROUPTHINK

Groupthink is a theory developed by an individual named Irving Janis in the 1970s, intended to describe faulty decision making that can occur in groups as a result of the forces that bring a group together. It's based on the common desire to not upset the balance of a group of people. It can, at times, mean favoring group consensus over common sense.

One famous example is Solomon Asch's line judgement experiment, where his goal was to measure the number of times each participant conformed to the majority view of which line best matched the "target line". Keep in mind, the length of the lines were obvious, as noted by this image.

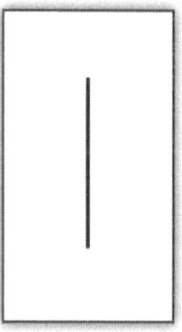 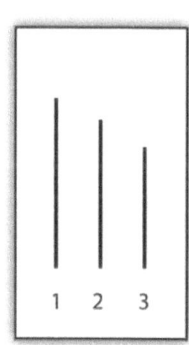

- Asch measured the number of times each participant conformed to the majority view. He found that, on average, about one third (32%) of the participants who were placed in this situation went along and conformed with the clearly incorrect majority on the critical trials.
- Over the 12 critical trials where the confederates (the participants that agreed to answer as Asch dictated) didn't make the obvious correct choice, about 75% of participants conformed at least once, and 25% of participants never conformed.
- In the control group, with no pressure to conform to confederates, less than 1% of participants gave the wrong answer.

His findings? People conform for two main reasons: because they want to fit in with the group (technical term: normative influence) and because they believe the group is better informed than they are (technical term: informational influence).

When the participants were interviewed after the experiment, most of them said that they did not really believe their conforming answers, but had gone along with the group for fear of being ridiculed, teased, or made fun of.

A few of them said that they really did believe the group's answers were correct.

WHY ARE WE TALKING ABOUT GROUPTHINK?

I've included groupthink in this section because it's important to recognize how others can influence our own behaviors. Even if we think we know what the right answer is, 75% of the time we defer to the group out of fear of becoming the "outcast." It is a protection mechanism, a product of our brain's biology, that preserves us and ensures our survival. Remember fight/flight/freeze? In instances like these, we tend to freeze and go with the flow rather than put up a fight or run away.

In a way, this experience is a study about loyalty. If you want to measure loyalty, people believing an absurdity is a far better test than when they go against the group, even when it's in favor of the truth. Ironic, but real.

> EVEN IF WE THINK WE KNOW WHAT THE RIGHT ANSWER IS, 75% OF THE TIME WE DEFER TO THE GROUP OUT OF FEAR OF BECOMING THE "OUTCAST."

UNCONSCIOUS BIAS

Over the last several years, the term "unconscious bias" has permeated through corporate culture and become a topic of interest for human resources and diversity and inclusion professionals alike. (Though the concept itself has been researched for many years in labs and social experiments—at least since 1954, when Gordon Allport published *On The Nature of Prejudice,* which established the theoretical foundations for the study of prejudice itself.) Trainings abound for the corporate professional of how to identify and gain awareness of these biases, and how to reduce their impact on decision-making in the workplace.

THE MIND IS JUST LIKE A MUSCLE

Remember the marvel that is the human brain. Our brains can consciously process 40 pieces of information per second. At the same time, we are unconsciously processing 11 million pieces. In an effort to keep pace with all of the stimuli around us—stimuli that seems to be growing daily with all the notifications, pings, and bings we receive on our phones and wearables—we create mental shortcuts that theoretically make decision-making easier. Unfortunately, though, many of these shortcuts actually highlight the biases ingrained in our brains and show up in our behaviors.

> We create mental shortcuts that theoretically make decision-making easier. Unfortunately, though, many of these shortcuts actually highlight the biases ingrained in our brains and show up in our behaviors.

Unconscious biases are learned stereotypes that are biological, unintentional, deeply ingrained, universal, and able to influence behavior.

How can a behavior be *learned* (nurture) but also biological (nature)?

Unconscious biases are social stereotypes about certain groups of people that individuals form outside their own conscious awareness. Everyone holds unconscious beliefs about various social and identity groups, and these biases stem from one's tendency to organize social worlds by categorizing. (Recall the idea of binaries and dualities from the introduction.)

Unconscious bias is far more prevalent than conscious prejudice, and is often incompatible with one's conscious values. Certain scenarios can activate unconscious attitudes and beliefs. For example, biases may be more prevalent when multi-tasking or working under time pressure.

Let's look at some types of unconscious bias and how they might present themselves in someone's behavior.

HALO EFFECT

In the 1920s, psychologist Edward Thorndike found that people who think highly of an individual in a specific context are likely to think highly of them in other ways as well. For example, if we find someone attractive, we'll probably also think they are intelligent and charismatic. Thorndike described this as the "halo effect," referring to the glowing circle of light surrounding an angel's crown. Basically, if we gravitate towards a person for one reason, we'll likely favor them in other ways, too. This kind of generalization can be dangerous, as rationalizing or dismissing warning signs of "bad behavior" can lead to unfavorable consequences.

For example, a manager assessing an employee's performance during review time should be wary of generalizing that performance. They need to consider that just because someone might have done an A-plus job on a project six months ago, doesn't necessarily mean that person is still contributing as effectively. If the manager succumbs to the halo effect, that manager may give the employee a "free pass," resulting in potentially reduced company productivity and resentment across the team.

Another relatable example are celebrities. Sometimes when we like a prominent figure because of their acting, philanthropic efforts, etc., we assume they are holistically good people. Consider Michael Jackson. Since his death in 2009, Jackson has been immortalized as the King of Pop and credited as the person who changed the way music videos were made. This is the same person that was riddled with allegations of child molestation and criticism of his increasingly eccentric lifestyle. There is a dissonance between how we thought of him throughout his life, and how he is remembered today. MJ is not unique in this regard; often, a person's character is perceived in a more positive light after their death. (There are few exceptions to this rule, i.e. Hitler.) It seems that because we have a tendency to view people holistically, if a person had any glimmer of a halo while they were here, we revel in their glory once they become our dearly departed.

CONFIRMATION BIAS

Once we make a decision or opinion about something, we tend to look for information that confirms our beliefs and overlook information that goes against them. This is a result of confirmation bias. Generally, people believe what they want to believe. For better or for worse, these preferences are reinforced throughout our day to day lives, whether we're aware of them or not.

Filter Bubbles

Your search engine (Google, for most of the planet) ensures that you only see results that you are interested in. If you and another person search for a term at the same moment, the

Internet's individualized algorithms can provide different results to each of you. Each time you click, you are influencing the subsequent advertisements and news recommendations that come your way. (Incognito Mode can help address this inherent bias, for those who are curious in testing it.) Netflix does this, too. The thumbnails of shows or movies each of us see vary from person to person, depending on the results of A/B testing that optimizes viewership. Crazy, right? In a sense, everything is curated in one way or another. How else would we navigate so much information?

Social Media

In a similar vein, we tend to surround ourselves with people and ideas with whom we share beliefs. This also applies to our digital communities on social media. It's highly likely you and most of your social media friends and followers share similar positions and views on issues. Your feeds likely consist of articles that reinforce what you believe, which you then repost for additional people to read. They click the "like" button and make comments you agree with.

If someone posts an opposing or (in your view) offensive opinion, you may either block or unfollow that person. I challenge you to add individuals, celebrities, world leaders, etc. that possess views contrary or different to your own if you don't follow them already, for the sake of broadening your exposure to the varying perspectives that exist in our world. It's a great exercise in awareness. We'll share other things you can do to widen your lens in Part III.

BROPRIATING

While I know the term "bropriating" isn't a technical term or well documented in academia, I came across it in my research for this book and think it's worth mentioning. The concept is this: In a group meeting, a female member of the team makes a point that no one seems to feel too strongly about. Thirty minutes later, a male member of the team makes the same point—and everyone jumps on board with "his" idea.

Throughout my ten years working in a corporate setting, I've witnessed this phenomenon first hand and heard anecdotes from female business people describing this kind of behavior. While the intent behind this behavior may not be malicious, this behavior can be harmful in the long run for female employees, resulting in reduced compensation, less internal recognition, and a slowed pace of promotion as compared to male counterparts.

There are many other unconscious biases, or heuristics, as referenced in psychology, that affect how we experience and interpret the world. For now, the takeaway is to be aware that they exist and there are things we can do to reduce their impact on our behaviors and therefore our choices, and in the long run, society at large.

PSYCHOLOGICAL PROJECTION

Psychological projection involves projecting undesirable feelings or emotions onto someone else, rather than admitting to or dealing with the unwanted feelings yourself. Psychological projection is a defense mechanism that people use to cope with feelings or emotions that don't feel good.

This concept was developed by Sigmund Freud, who is often referred to as the "Father of Psychoanalysis." During his sessions with patients, Freud noticed a pattern: Sometimes, patients would accuse others of having the same feelings the patients themselves were demonstrating.

By engaging in this behavior, the patient was better able to deal with the emotions he or she was experiencing.

Have you ever come in contact with other people who "hate" or "dislike" you for no reason? While we are convinced that the words, tone, and glances given to us are reflections of a deep dislike, most of the time, we fail to realize that believing someone "hates us" is often actually a result of projection. If we have a strong dislike for someone in the first place, it is common for us to protect ourselves against this feeling by projecting it onto another. Has this happened to you recently? Think about someone you don't like. What don't you like about them? Is that thing something in yourself you don't like, or maybe even feel shame about?

The most common one for people across all ages is the fear that your partner/boyfriend/girlfriend/significant other is having an affair or is untrustworthy. This can often be a reflection of the way you feel about yourself. All normal people functioning in relationships feel attracted to other people at one point or another, and sometimes this self-discovery is met with fear and shame, which is then often projected onto the other partner.

Shame can play a powerful role in psychological projection, often accompanying jealousy or resentment. Exploring these underlying issues within ourselves helps us identify and fix the behavior.

I mention psychological projection in this section because, at the individual level, it can play a defining role in how we engage with others, especially if we're not aware of it. If not acknowledged, it can run rampant and plague relationships on many levels, including within our families, with friends and peers, and at school.

Psychological projection isn't a bias, per se, but it exists as a result of nuances in the brain that "protect" us from negative feelings. Whereas often, in today's world, it is actually better in the long run to feel your feelings than protect yourself from them. (Sure, in hunter-gatherer days, it was probably better to protect ourselves from having negative feelings because our ancestors were reliant on very few people for survival, and it was probably best not to make them angry.) To feel your feelings is to accept your feelings. Remember the awareness/acceptance duality? Becoming aware of psychological projection and accepting the terms around which it takes place is the root of making peace with your thoughts and building awareness. What we don't know scares us. If we know, we have less opportunity to feel fear and shame.

THE INTERNET EFFECT

The term "internet effect" as used here is a reference to the consequences of the latest revolutionary technologies—namely, the internet— on how humans think.

How we consume information has evolved as a result of inventions, advancements, and changes such as the printing press, the television, and most recently, the internet. Human history can be time stamped in three revolutions:

1. The Cognitive Revolution
2. The Agricultural Revolution
3. The Scientific Revolution

We could say that we are still living in the Scientific Revolution. During this era, we have witnessed the birth of the internet and its immediate consequences. To make it simple, let's say the internet started making a notable impact beginning in 2000. If we assume that anyone born in the Generation Z demographic (born between 1997-2012) and later "grew up with the internet," we're talking about 23% of the American population. If we assume anyone born in the Generation Y demographic (born between 1981-1996) and later "grew up with the internet," we're talking about 47% of the American population. For Gen Y, the internet became a daily feature around high school or college; for Gen Z, it was elementary or middle school—very different yet formative periods in a lifetime. Of today's living population in America, about half grew up with the internet. Today, 50% of 11 year-olds have their own cell phone.

Social media is a by-product of the internet, as are many products and services available to us in the forms of devices (I see you, Apple) and ecommerce platforms (Amazon). Once might even call these inventions "distractions". As Nicholas Carr describes it in his book on this topic, Shallows: What the Internet Is Doing to Our Brains,

"The distractions in our lives have been proliferating for a long time, but never has there been a medium that, like the Net, has been programmed to so widely scatter our attention and to do it so insistently."

A vulnerability of human psychology is centered around this impulse, our innate human need for gratification. Social media platforms, like the long-gone Myspace and the more long-standing (i.e. still surviving) Facebook, Instagram, Twitter, and Youtube (and more recently still, TikTok), are great examples of this, but there are other more "useful" technologies that also exploit this human weakness.

Consider the GPS. While helpful for navigation, there are times when these systems break down: they don't have sufficient mapping capabilities; the address is incorrect and you wind up somewhere else

THE MIND IS JUST LIKE A MUSCLE

unintentionally; it says to make a U-turn when you know you can just go left and arrive at your destination.

The point is, we have these great, complex brains, and yet sometimes we let things take advantage of them and override their capabilities and strengths. The challenge is having the awareness to realize when this is happening, and adjust accordingly. In a word, exercise.

> "THE DISTRACTIONS IN OUR LIVES HAVE BEEN PROLIFERATING FOR A LONG TIME, BUT NEVER HAS THERE BEEN A MEDIUM THAT, LIKE THE NET, HAS BEEN PROGRAMMED TO SO WIDELY SCATTER OUR ATTENTION AND TO DO IT SO INSISTENTLY."

It's also possible that the depth of our intelligence is shifting. Humans used to define intelligence as the extent to which a person had a mind capable of sitting quietly and solving complex problems. However, after the Industrial Revolution, a new definition of intelligence started to take hold—one that privileged efficiency and multitasking over deep thinking. We can think about these types of intelligence 1) as shallow and wide, and 2) narrow and deep. With the invention of the internet, our obsession with efficiency has spiraled out of control. Our applications, platforms, and digital tools are so quick and easy to use that we have become obsessed with being better, faster, stronger—but at what cost? The volume of data we are exposed to when we surf the web may be impressive, but our brains are not equipped to both navigate the distractions inherent in the design of the internet and consolidate deep and meaningful new elements of knowledge. Increased reliance on the internet has induced what can be called "an age of distraction," resulting in our own inability to find a balance between being thoughtful and solutions-oriented and fast and efficient, in a world now dictated by the computer and its accessories.

Consider that there are now entire careers devoted to this. User experience, or UX, design is just one. 85% of jobs that will exist in 2030 haven't even been invented yet. That's a direct result of the speed at which technology changes how we approach and perform work. (I've written quite a few blog posts on this topic. Please see the Appendix for a few selections about the future of work.)

As with psychological projection, the internet effect isn't a bias, but it exposes limitations of the human brain that can result in less-than-optimum consequen-ces if we're not mindful of how to manage its impact.

> WE HAVE THESE GREAT, COMPLEX BRAINS, AND YET SOMETIMES WE LET THINGS TAKE ADVANTAGE OF THEM AND OVERRIDE THEIR CAPABILITIES AND STRENGTHS. THE CHALLENGE IS HAVING THE AWARENESS TO REALIZE WHEN THIS IS HAPPENING, AND ADJUST ACCORDINGLY. IN A WORD, EXERCISE.

THE BRAIN IS JUST LIKE A MUSCLE

Based on the research, bias may be natural to us, but our consciousness gives us the benefit of awareness if we're willing to exercise our brains. After all, the brain is more than a keeper of intelligence. The brain is just like a muscle. Building awareness is like building muscle—only in our cranium, and not on our biceps. It's a

THE MIND IS JUST LIKE A MUSCLE

strength that will help us in the long run. If we don't maintain it, it will atrophy and go limp.

How do our brains affect our dynamics inside our households? Our relationships with our parents, our siblings, our caretakers? In the next section, we will explore what those family dynamics can look like and how to be mindful of their dynamics.

PART II: INSIDE & OUTSIDE THE HOUSEHOLD

At this point, we've learned A LOT about the brain and how its structure affects the way we see the world. In short, we learned our brain is inherently biased. We went through examples of how these biases play out, from historical examples to our Google search queries.

We also learned (or reminded ourselves) that the brain is just like a muscle, and as such, it needs exercise to get stronger.

How do we not succumb to the way our brains have evolved to program our behaviors? By building awareness, and practicing acceptance, i.e., exercise.

In this section, we'll consider these insights as we zero in on the household, which is (for many of us) the core of our day-to-day life and where we put down our roots. I'm using the term "household" here to describe the people and relationships that shape our upbringings during childhood, until or around age 18. I realize that's not consistent for everyone. To tell this story, I'm referring to well-documented and researched findings from well-reputed academic institutions. Even then, the findings are only as good as their inputs. Remember, life happens on a continuum, and there are always varying degrees of execution.

For this section, we will share research findings that focus on relationship dynamics between parents, siblings, and the greater family structure. There are *lots* of studies referenced. Don't be overwhelmed! The idea is to use these studies to shed light on household dynamics through a variety of lenses, as life is far from one-dimensional.

INSIDE THE HOUSEHOLD

Family dynamics vary across households. That's a fact. Every family system is unique. There are too many variables that affect how a family unit functions for there to be measurable sameness on every dimension.

I myself grew up in a nuclear family—with a mom, a dad, a sister, and a brother. For a long time, I thought everyone did. Until I went to elementary school, where five out of six of the girls in my friend group came from blended families (yes, I was the sixth). Throughout most of human history, families resided in multigenerational households, which consist of the aforementioned nuclear family, plus grandparents, cousins, children of the nuclear family's children, etc.

Today, only a minority of American households are traditional two-parent nuclear families and only one-third of American individuals live in this kind of family. The nuclear family existed in a post-World War II time where multiple forces created a perfect storm of circumstances that allowed this type of family unit to flourish. At a high level, aside from this

1950-1965 period, the nuclear family hasn't been the most common form of familial structure in American history. (This is a good time to remember America is only 250 years old. The youngest country in the world today is South Sudan, which became official in 2011.) Let's take a closer look.

A BRIEF RECENT HISTORY OF AMERICAN FAMILY STRUCTURES

In 1800, just barely 25 years after the American Revolution, 75 percent of American workers were farmers. Most of the other quarter worked in small family businesses. As factories opened in the big U.S. cities during the Industrial Revolution in the late 19th and early 20th centuries, young people left home to pursue their own goals, i.e. the American Dream. Improved food production methods decreased the need for farm labor. Therefore, children were no longer being groomed to work on their family farms. They were raised to become independent, to build their own families. During this period, the average marriage age dropped for both men and women: 3.6 years for men and 2.2 years for women—in many cases from the mid-20s to the early 20s.

By the 1920s, the "farming family" was all but replaced by the nuclear family. By 1960, almost 80 percent of all children were living with their two married parents in separate households from their extended family.

Starting in the mid 70s, young men's wages declined. People put greater value on privacy and autonomy. A rising feminist movement helped women gain greater degrees of freedom to choose their work and life dispositions. (Progress, yet there's still much to be done.)

Perhaps as a result, Americans today have less family than ever before. From 1970 to 2012, the number of households with married couples and their kids dropped by 50 percent. In 1960, only 13 percent of all households were single-person households, as compared to 28 percent in 2018.

In 1850, 75 percent of Americans older than 65 lived with relatives, whereas in 1990, only 18 percent did. It will be interesting to see how this figure changes, with Baby Boomers (people born between 1946 and 1964) now reaching this age bracket. These are also the folks who grew up when the nuclear family unit was on the rise.

Married Versus Single

Over the past two generations, people have spent less and less time in marriage, marrying later, if at all, and divorcing more. In 1950, 27 percent of marriages ended in divorce. That number is 45 percent today. In 1960, only 28 percent of American adults were single. In 2017, nearly 50 percent of American adults were single. According to a 2014 report from the Urban Institute, roughly 90 percent of Baby Boomer women and 80 percent of Gen X women (born between 1965 and 1980) were married by age 40. About 70 percent of late-Millennial women (born in the early 90s) were expected to do so, which is the lowest rate in U.S. history to date. In 2004, 33 percent of Americans ages 18 to 34 were living without a romantic partner. In 2018, that number was up to 51 percent.

Families have also gotten a lot smaller over the past few decades. The average American birth rate is half of what it was in 1960. In 2012, most American family households had no children. There are more American homes with pets than with kids. (That just blows my mind.)

College Kids

Especially since the 2008 recession, economic pressures have pushed Americans toward greater reliance on family. Starting around 2012, the share of children living with married parents began to inch up. College students also rely on their parents more than they did a generation ago, because the educational process is longer and more expensive. (Side note: education itself may evolve and change in the coming decades, as technology replaces skills only humans once had, and preparation for the workforce may need an update to meet the terms of how society defines "work.")

Multigenerational Households

The financial crisis of 2008 prompted a sharp rise in multigenerational homes. Today 20 percent of Americans—64 million people, an all-time high—live in multigenerational homes. In 1980, that figure was only 12 percent.

The return of the extended family as a common family structure was triggered by young adults moving back home. In 2014, 35 percent of American men ages 18 to 34 lived with their parents. Polling reports suggest that many young people are looking ahead to helping their parents when they reach a certain age. In fact, the percentage of seniors who live alone reached a high around 1990. Now more than 20 percent of Americans 65 and over live in multigenerational homes. (This doesn't include the large share of seniors who are moving to be close to their grandkids but not into the same household.)

Sliced another way, more than 20 percent of Asians, black people, and Latinos live in multigenerational households, compared with 16 percent of white people.

REDEFINING KINSHIP

For many periods throughout human history, people lived in extended families made up of not just people they were related to, but people they chose to cooperate with. An international research team found that a group of people who were buried together around 34,000 years ago in what is now modern Russia were not closely related to one another. In a study of 32 present-day foraging societies, primary kin—parents, siblings, and children—usually made up less than 10 percent of a residential band, or village type structure. Extended families in traditional societies may or may not have been genetically close, but they probably had more intimate relationships. You could look at these bands as the early version of blended families.

Going a step further, there's evidence to suggest 80% of early human societies were considered polygamous by definition: polygyny, in which a man has more than one wife, and polyandry, in which a woman has more than one husband. Today, polygamy is illegal in the United States. (You might be familiar with the TLC show "Sister Wives." How do they get around the law? In short, while having multiple marriage licenses is considered illegal, cohabitation is not.)

Aside: Why didn't polygamy last and how did it come to be illegal in America? That's another story. Many countries in the world today still practice and accept polygamy as a standard family unit. Though, anecdotally, many people prefer not to have more than one spouse. Why? Polygamy is expensive.

What can we take away from this? There are many dimensions involved in defining a family, and every family is unique. As we've learned, the family unit has evolved tremendously throughout history, arguably more so in the last century than during any other period in human history, at least in America. A 2009 study shows that family structure is no longer decisive in a young person's perception of proper family function. "At the start of the study, teenagers from nuclear families had a better perception of family function, but this has changed to become equal with those of other family structures," explains the expert.

When you think of your close friends, your classmates, consider how their experiences at home might be different from yours. Just be aware that this is most likely the case. How does that change your relationship with them? Noodle on it and let me know (bysarasalam.com/contact).

There's definitely hope. Many of us are educating ourselves and each other about our families. As we noted earlier, as of January 2019, over 26 million people had taken an ancestry test. Two of those people were my brother and sister. (If you are curious, the results were the same.) This curiosity is extremely important, not only for the future of research and study, but for ourselves and each other as we navigate this increasingly interconnected world, where the probability that we will encounter things that are unfamiliar to us is quite high.

A CLOSER LOOK: LATINO CULTURES

I grew up in Southern California, which has a high percentage of Latino residents. The Hispanic/Latino population in the United States in 2018 was 59.9 million, or about 18% of the total population.

One of the most common questions is, who is considered Hispanic in the United States? And how are they (or any demographic group, for that matter) counted in public opinion surveys, voter exit polls, and government surveys like the census? This is the same for any race and/or ethnicity. I chose this particular one as a case study because it shows just how complex classifying races and/or ethnicities is.

THE MIND IS JUST LIKE A MUSCLE

The most common approach to answering the first question (who is considered Hispanic?) is straightforward: Anyone who says they are. And nobody who says they aren't.

Most research organizations, including the U.S. Census Bureau and Pew Research, use this method to estimate this data. This is the method the Census Bureau used to estimate there were roughly 59.9 million Hispanics in the United States as of July 1, 2018.

Keep in mind there is a long history of changing labels, shifting categories and revised question wording on census forms. As definitions evolve and change, so do the data.

Below is the Census Bureau's approach of using self-identification to decide who is Hispanic, as reference from a Pew Research article on gathering data on who is Hispanic.

Q. I immigrated to Phoenix from Mexico. Am I Hispanic?

A. You are if you say so.

Q. My parents moved to New York from Puerto Rico. Am I Hispanic?

A. You are if you say so.

Q. My grandparents were born in Spain but I grew up in California. Am I Hispanic?

A. You are if you say so.

Q. I was born in Maryland and married an immigrant from El Salvador. Am I Hispanic?

A. You are if you say so.

Q. I was born in Argentina but grew up in Texas. I don't consider myself Hispanic. Does the Census Bureau count me as Hispanic?

A. Not if you say you aren't. Of the 42.7 million adults with Hispanic ancestry in 2015, an estimated 5 million people, or 11%, said they do not identify as Hispanic or Latino. These people aren't counted as Hispanic by the Census Bureau or in Pew Research Center surveys.

Hispanic self-identification varies across immigrant generations. Among the foreign born from Latin America, nearly all self-identify as Hispanic. But by the fourth generation, only half of people with Hispanic heritage in the U.S. self-identify as Hispanic.

Q: But isn't there an official definition of what it means to be Hispanic or Latino?

A: In 1976, U.S. Congress passed the only law in this country's history that mandated the collection and analysis of data for a specific ethnic group: "Americans of Spanish origin or descent." The language of that legislation described this group as "Americans who identify themselves as being of Spanish-speaking background and trace their origin or descent from Mexico, Puerto Rico, Cuba, Central and South America, and other Spanish-speaking countries." This includes 20 Spanish-speaking nations from Latin America and Spain itself, but not Portugal or Portuguese-speaking Brazil. Standards for collecting data on Hispanics were developed by the Office of Management and Budget (OMB) in 1977 and revised in 1997. Using these standards, schools, public health facilities, and other government entities and agencies keep track of how many Hispanics they serve—the primary goal of the 1976 law.

However, the Census Bureau does not apply this definition when counting Hispanics. Rather, it relies entirely on self-reporting and lets each person identify as Hispanic or not.

According to another study published in 2010, Latinos represent more than 20 different groups, and they live in very different situations in the United States. Notice this is an attempt to categorize or classify groups of people based on shared variables, like country of origin, language, religion, etc. I share this with you to remind us that everyone's baseline is different, including how we define categories and their parameters.

For example, Cuban immigrants who moved to the United States when Castro came to power tended to be very wealthy, and they created an entrepreneurial, successful enclave in Miami. Compare them with Central American immigrants who may be refugees from a civil war in the 1980s. Language, religion, and some aspects of culture are apt to be the same, but socioeconomic status is probably very different.

What about behaviors influenced by cultural norms or expectations? In traditional Latin cultures, *machismo* dictates that men be, well, *macho*— meaning that they are strong and provide for their family. In the United States, when we say macho, often we mean someone's a male chauvinist, but in most Latin cultures, this idea encompasses such positive behavior as being responsible for your family and taking care of your household.

The female ideal of *marianismo* includes being self-sacrificing, pure, and silent. But the researcher emphasized that few studies have tried to measure the extent to which Latinos adhere to these traditional gender roles and whether cultural beliefs are linked to sexual behavior.

One member of the research team noted most research on Latino gender roles and sexuality doesn't take into account that Latin cultures have changed tremendously over the last 20 years as a result of globalization, migration, and changing norms.

Immigrant status also plays a role in teens' sexual risk taking. Research findings suggest that for first-generation Latinos, recent immigration seems to be a protective factor. Families tend to bring the practices they had in their home country, and there's a shift as they become acculturated over time. For girls, being an immigrant is protective because Latin American countries are typically more conservative about sexuality than the United States is.

For boys, the opposite pattern may be true, because in many Latin American countries men have more freedom to explore their sexuality. In the United States, they might shift to a more conservative pattern.

From this example, we can see how fluid the idea of ethnic identity is within the Hispanic and Latino cultures. It illustrates how our human brains use categorization to help us make sense of the world, including our identities. However, there is always more than meets the eye. As citizens of a global society, we need to do a better job of educating ourselves about the people and world around us, develop awareness around them, and proceed accordingly.

PARENTS

In my research, I came across this anecdote by an academic named Dr. Insoo. It highlights how culture can be a filter for our conceptions of what is "correct," even when it comes to parenting.

Dr. Insoo, a Korean immigrant, was confused about how the parents disciplined their teenage child in the wake of a conflict via "grounding":

THE MIND IS JUST LIKE A MUSCLE

The parents explained that when their child disobeyed them, they punished their child by making them stay in the house. Unfortunately, this explanation puzzled Insoo . . . because in Korean culture, it is considered an honor to be in the house spending time with your family, and many times children are expected to live with and take care of their aging parents. Insoo was confused by the idea that to punish the child, the parents forced the child to stay in the house with the parents. This parenting technique seemed incongruous to Insoo, who was coming from a Korean perspective.

In this example, we see the effects of ethnocentrism at play. Remember, ethnocentrism is the use of one's own culture as the standard to judge other cultures. It's the assumption that one's own culture is the natural order of things and the "correct" way to live, the center of everything. Now, we don't know from this anecdote if Insoo believes the Korean culture is objectively the center of the universe. That's not the point. The point is in Insoo's confusion around parenting style. Why is she confused? Because she is unfamiliar with the approach her (Caucasian) clients take when it comes to disciplining their child. Remember, what we don't know scares us. Insoo's frame of reference is different from that of her clients. If something is unfamiliar, our brains fire in a certain way (recall our deep-dive in Part I about the brain). But we can also make conscious decisions regarding how we behave.

This story comes from the preface of *Solution-focused Brief Therapy: A Multicultural Approach,* written about the multicultural approach to solutions-based brief therapy. It was written specifically with the intent to acknowledge and address how the interaction of multiple cultural backgrounds can result in conflicting viewpoints, and how to move past these conflicts in a productive way. In a nutshell, this story is predicated on awareness and acceptance. When we acknowledge that differences exist, we can foster conversations around why that is and how we can recognize the ways these differences affect our realities and perceptions of reality.

Whether we're aware of it or not, parents play a key role in the development of their kids' identity. One study acknowledges that mainstream belief regarding identity theory tends to portray adolescents as the only variable involved in their identity development. However, these findings show that parents are concerned, involved, and reflective participants in their children's identity formation.

And so, we shouldn't be surprised at the extent to which our parents influence us throughout our youth, and the implications beyond our youth. Though we may be surprised about which "parental variables" have the most impact on us.

Let's explore some of them.

Same-Sex and Different-Sex Parents

A study published in 2018 finds that children of both same-sex and different-sex parents both fare well in terms of psychological adjustment throughout their upbringings. Meaning, the sex of their parents did not affect the kids' development from a psychological standpoint.

The study was conducted in Italy amongst three groups of parents: 70 gay fathers who had children through surrogacy, 125 lesbian mothers who had children through donor insemination, and 195 heterosexual couples who had children through spontaneous conception. The children were 3 to 11 years old, and the groups were matched for child characteristics.

Overall, children of same-sex parents fewer reported difficulties than children of different-sex parents. The researchers note that scores were in the normal range (statiscally) for all three groups. Normal range in this case means the difficulties or lack thereof were not extreme, in either case.

They found that family structure is not predictive of child health outcomes once family process variables are taken into account.

Suffice it to say, parenting is less about the gender of the parents and more about the functional family unit the parents are responsible for leading.

Family Structure

Moreover, the structure or composition of the family isn't the key—it's the family dynamic itself.

The results of the 2009 study show that family structure is no longer decisive in a kid's perception of proper family function. "At the start of the study, teenagers from nuclear families had a better perception of family function, but this has changed to become equal with those of other family structures," explains the expert.

Previous studies pointed to families without a regular structure (headed by a lone parent, or other family members such as grandparents or uncles, or including the children of other partners, etc.) leading to a greater risk of teenagers living in such families turning to drugs or being violent, having mental health problems, or even exhibiting criminal behavior.

According to the study, this is not the case.

Older teenagers (ages 16 to 18) have improved their perception of family functionality, regardless of factors such as family structure or gender, which the authors of the study believe may be related to the progressive delay in their leaving home.

"However, social reality shows that family structure has changed over recent years, with families with different structures being increasingly common," points out one of the authors. "During adolescence, families should focus on promoting a positive family dynamic, regardless of their structure".

And so, as we learned earlier about the large irrelevance of the nuclear family in today's world, structure is less important than dynamic.

> AS WE LEARNED EARLIER ABOUT THE LARGE IRRELEVANCE OF THE NUCLEAR FAMILY IN TODAY'S WORLD, STRUCTURE IS LESS IMPORTANT THAN DYNAMIC.

Mapping modern family dynamics on Facebook

A recent study by research scientists at Facebook analyzed 400,000 Facebook posts to determine differences in how parents talk to their children versus other friends and how they address their adult versus teen children. The posts, stripped of identifiable user information, showed that children's communication with their parents decreases in frequency from age 13 on, but then rises when they move out. Counter to previous research on familial communication, they also found that living farther away from each other does not diminish how much parents and children talk on Facebook.

The study also found differences between how mothers and fathers use Facebook. Automatic language coding showed that mothers' posts showed more emotion, using phrases like "poor baby" or "so proud of," while fathers' posts were more abstract, with phrases such as "keep it up" or "got your back." Also, mothers were more likely to ask children to call them, while fathers talked more about shared interests, such as politics or sports.

Going forward, it will be interesting to see how social media continues to reflect or change how parents and their children engage with each other (or not).

DISCIPLINE

When I use the word "structure," I'm referring to roles or positions within a family unit. Discipline, on the other hand, is about setting boundaries and instituting a framework that describes those boundaries and enforces them. I often hear adults say, "My kids need structure." I don't know if I agree with that statement in isolation. I think kids need boundaries, and the freedom to discover and live within those boundaries. Full disclosure: I don't have kids, but I was one once, and looking back, I can assuredly say that's what worked for me.

Siblings

How does a family dynamic change when multiple kids are in the mix? What if you have siblings? A study by the Society for Research in Child Development found that treating children differently within a family can result in divisive family dynamics. When siblings within the same family were parented very differently, all children in those families showed more mental health problems.

Parents act differently with different children—for example, being more positive with one child and more negative with another. A study looking at almost 400 Canadian families has found that this behavior negatively affects not only the child who receives more negative feedback, but all the children in the family. The study also found that the more risks experienced by parents, the more likely they will treat their children differentially.

For example, mothers with a lot of risk factors (such as single parenting, low income, past abuse, or lack of safety at home) were found to be more differential in how they treated their children than moms whose lives were less stressful. Such cumulative risk has been associated with increased mental health problems in children, such as aggression, attention, and emotional problems.

What's more, even the number of siblings itself could impact the likelihood of divorce for the children themselves. More siblings means more experience dealing with others, and that seems to provide additional help in dealing with a marriage relationship as an adult. The practical difference between having no siblings and having one or two isn't that much in terms of divorce. But by the same token, when you compare children from large families to those with only one child, there is a meaningful gap in the probability of divorce.

The researchers analyzed a variety of variables, of both the respondents they surveyed and their parents, that could have played a role in future divorces, including education, socioeconomic status, family structure, race, age at marriage, whether the respondents had children, gender role attitudes, and religious affiliation, among others.

THE MIND IS JUST LIKE A MUSCLE

When they added in all of these controls, nothing took away the relationship they saw between siblings and later divorce. None of these other factors explained it away.

As the study suggests, when you grow up in a family with siblings, you develop a set of skills for negotiating both negative and positive interactions. You have to consider other people's points of view, learn how to talk through problems. The more siblings you have, the more opportunities you have to practice those skills. That can be a good foundation for adult relationships, including marriage.

This new study is an attempt to both examine the effect of siblings later in life and to see how it impacts more major life events, which is different compared to most other studies on the subject.

Evaluations of social skills and grades aren't trivial, but divorce is a more concrete, consequential event in a person's life. This is the first study to look at how siblings affect such a consequential event in adulthood.

When it comes to discipline, how far is too far?

A study of 967 two-parent families and their children has found that harsh verbal discipline, defined as the psychological force causing emotional pain or discomfort to correct or control behavior, in early adolescence can be harmful to teens later.

The children of mothers and fathers who used harsh verbal discipline when they were 13 suffered more depressive symptoms between ages 13 and 14 than their peers who weren't disciplined in this way. They were also more likely to have conduct problems, such as misbehaving at school, lying to parents, stealing, or fighting.

In addition, the study found not only does harsh verbal discipline appear to be ineffective at addressing behavior problems in youths, it also appears to exacerbate such behaviors.

The effect went the other way, too. Children who had conduct problems at 13 elicited more harsh verbal discipline from their parents between ages 13 and 14.

"This is one of the first studies to indicate that parents' harsh verbal discipline is damaging to the developing adolescent," says the leader of the study. "The notion that harsh discipline is without consequence, once there is a strong parent-child bond—that the adolescent will understand that 'they're doing this because they love me'—is misguided because parents' warmth didn't lessen the effects of harsh verbal discipline.

"Indeed, harsh verbal discipline appears to be detrimental in all circumstances," she concludes.

Ultimately, when parents seek to modify their teen's behavior, a better approach might be discussions around the consequences and their related concerns, rather than harsh verbal discipline.

LOVE

What's love got to do with it? A study conducted of Nepalese families found that love between parents correlates to children staying in school longer and marrying later in life.

"In this study, we saw that parents' emotional connection to each other affects child rearing so much that it shapes their children's future," said the co-author. "The fact that we found these kinds of things in Nepal moves us step closer to evidence that these things are universal."

In Nepal, parents historically arranged their children's marriage, and divorce was rare. Since the 1970s, more couples have married for love, and while divorce is still rare, it is becoming more common.

Education has also become more common since the 1970s. By grade 10, children can take an exam to earn their "School-Leaving Certificate." The increase in SLC's across both genders is noteworthy. Data shows fewer than 3% of ever-married women aged 15-49 had earned an SLC in 1996, while nearly 25% of women earned an SLC in 2016. Thirty-one percent of men earned SLCs in 2011. By 2016, 36.8% of men had.

Even after consideration of other potentially influential factors—including caste-ethnicity; access to schools; whether the parents had an arranged marriage; the childbearing of the parents; and whether the parents had experience living outside their own families—these findings maintain their validity.

"Family isn't just another institution. It's not like a school or employer. It is this place where we also have emotions and feelings," said the lead author. "Demonstrating and providing evidence that love, this emotional component of family, also has this long impact on children's lives is really important for understanding the depth of family influence on children."

BULLYING

Elizabeth Sweeney, a University of Cincinnati master's degree student in sociology, conducted research for her Master's degree in 2008 about bullying and whether it's a hereditary phenomenon.

Her research found that children raised by authoritarian parents—i.e., parents who are demanding, directive and unresponsive—are the most likely to demonstrate what we recognize as bullying behavior. Concurrently, Sweeney also noticed that children raised by nurturing, warm, responsive parents were less likely to bully.

"Children who experience hostility, abuse, physical discipline, and other aggressive behaviors by their parents are more likely to model that behavior in their peer relationships," she writes. "Children learn from their parents how to behave and interact with others," Sweeney says. "So if they're learning about aggression and angry words at home, they will tend to use these behaviors as coping mechanisms when they interact with their peers." Her review also found that children from middle-income families were less likely to bully than children from the high and low ends of the family income scale.

She says that while some studies suggest boys are more prone to bullying than girls, others state that it runs equally among the genders, although boys are more likely to act out bullying physically, while girls are more verbal.

Sweeney adds that it is the tolerance of bullying that "has served as one of the primary contributors to its persistence and severity."

LEGACIES OF PARENTING

Parenting is hard. Sometimes, there are unintended consequences that happen from choice parenting styles. And sometimes parents aren't even aware a specific action might lead to a specific outcome—positive or negative.

For example, one study found that commitment-phobic adults likely learned this behavior from unresponsive or overbearing parenting, which seems like two poles on the opposite sides of the parenting spectrum. That's a lot of pressure.

Often, we don't know if something is bad until way later, when there is time to observe the effects. Not to mention humans are inherently bad at anticipating consequences, such as climate change, medications, or the internet. We're not very long-term thinkers by way of biology. Parenting is not immune to these circumstances. Here are some documented examples.

"Extreme Parenting"

A study of the romantic history of 58 adults aged 22-28 found that those who avoid committed romantic relationships are likely a product of unresponsive or over-intrusive parenting.

The premise of this study is based on attachment theory, which posits that during times of stress, infants seek proximity to their caregivers for emotional support. However, if the parent is unresponsive or overly intrusive, the child learns to avoid their caregiver.

The researchers believe that adult relationships reflect these earlier experiences. When infantile needs are met in childhood, that person approaches adult relationships with more security, seeking intimacy, sharing, caring, and fun.

When they enter relationships, there is an attempt to satisfy their unmet childhood needs. "Avoidant individuals are looking for somebody to validate them, accept them as they are, can consistently meet their needs and remain calm—including not making a fuss about anything or getting caught up in their own personal issues."

The tendency to avoid dependence on a partner is a defense mechanism rather than an avoidance of intimacy, she adds. This behavior also correlates with less happiness and a higher incidence of illness.

Helicopter Parenting

Helicopter parenting isn't done for what the child wants; it can be done for what the parent wants for the child.

One study suggests the phenomenon of helicopter parenting most often occurs in middle- to upper-class families, where stakes are high for parents to be able to show off their children's success. This research, which focuses on young adults 18 to 24 years old, indicates that high helicopter parenting leads to "low mastery, self-regulation and social competence."

A recent example of this is the college admissions scandal involving high profile celebrity parents falsifying school records supposedly for the benefit of their children.

The dichotomy does more harm than just resentment toward an interfering parent. Moilanen said children take parents' repeated over-involvement in their decisions to heart, undermining their sense of self-concept and their ability to self-regulate.

Children might figure out problems on their own, but the parent swoops in before they have the opportunity to learn for themselves. Collateral side effects of the child's continued lack of autonomy could be heightened anxiety and internalizing problems, as well as leading to the belief that they are incapable of living independently, and that their outcomes are primarily shaped by external forces instead of their own decisions, the research said.

As we've seen through the research, parenting is hard. Parenting in modern America is hard. The more we understand and are aware of the factors that play critical roles in our upbringings, we can make better decisions for our families and for ourselves.

OUTSIDE THE HOUSEHOLD

In the introduction, we mentioned how complex modern America is. Our country is young and dynamic. With that comes a lot of implications for the millions of people who call America home. In this section, we'll look at different ways to describe our population. Then, we'll look at the forces at play outside the household—such as the media, politics, and how these forces impact how we view each other and ourselves.

IMMIGRANTS

An immigrant is a person who comes to live permanently in a foreign country.

The United States has more immigrants than any other country in the world. Today, more than 40 million people living in the U.S. were born in another country, accounting for about 20% of the world's migrants in 2017. The population of immigrants is also very diverse, with just about every country in the world represented among U.S. immigrants.

Think about this. How incredible is it, the spectrum of diversity our country hosts? As we've learned in previous sections, when it comes to processing so much that's different, it can be overwhelming to our brains, to our ability to process. But if we make the effort to build awareness, we'll get better at processing over time. Remember, human biases in perception are malleable and subject to individual motivations and goals. Simply put, we can consciously make the effort to embrace people that are different from us, i.e., exercise our brains and embrace the diversity of modern America.

Stats to Note

Mexico is the top origin country of the U.S. immigrant population. In 2017, 11.2 million immigrants living in the U.S. were from Mexico, accounting for 25% of all U.S. immigrants. The next largest origin groups were those from China (6%), India (6%), the Philippines (5%), and El Salvador (3%).

Roughly half (45%) of the nation's 44.4 million immigrants live in just three states: California (24%), Texas (11%), and New York (10%). California had the largest immigrant population of any state in 2017, at 10.6 million. Texas and New York had more than 4.5 million immigrants each.

In 2017, most immigrants lived in just 20 major metropolitan areas, with the largest populations in New York, Los Angeles, and Miami.

More than 1 million immigrants arrive in the U.S. each year. In 2017, the top country of origin for new immigrants coming into the U.S. was India, with 126,000 people, followed by Mexico (124,000), China (121,000) and Cuba (41,000).

MULTICULTURAL INDIVIDUALS

In the 2010 U.S. census, approximately 9 million individuals, or 2.9% of the population, self-identified as multiracial. By 2015, one in seven U.S. infants (14%) were multiracial or multiethnic, nearly triple the share in 1980, according to a Pew Research Center analysis of Census Bureau data.

THE MIND IS JUST LIKE A MUSCLE

Multiracial or multiethnic infants include children less than 1 year old whose parents are each of a different race, those with one Hispanic and one non-Hispanic parent, and those with at least one parent who identifies as multiracial. (Remember our discussion about "Who is Hispanic?" earlier? This is another example of how classifying along racial and ethnic lines can get confusing. And it is confusing. But this is the information we have, and it's worth sharing.) This analysis is limited to infants living with two parents, because census data on the race and ethnicity of parents is only available for those living in the same home. In 2015, this was the case for 62% of all infants.

The rapid rise in the share of infants who are multiracial or multiethnic has occurred hand-in-hand with the growth in marriages among spouses of different races or ethnicities. In 1980, 7% of all newlyweds were in an intermarriage, and by 2015, that share had more than doubled to 17%, according to a recently released Pew Research Center report. Both trends are likely spurred in part by the growing racial and ethnic diversity in the U.S.

Studies have shown that kids who are adept at navigating different cultural contexts are better at taking the perspective of others and developing empathy. Embracing one's culture of origin connects children to a community of people, a set of values, and a sense of history, all of which help offset the negative effects of racism, discrimination, and poverty—realities that characterize our world today.

Kids with greater ties to their cultural identities are more likely to value and be motivated to succeed in school. When kids are encouraged to bring their languages and cultures into classrooms, all students benefit from learning from each other. It's important preparation for living in an increasingly global and diverse world. This is a great example of how building awareness and educating each other can result in a cooperative, inclusive environment.

Multiculturalism is not new

Multiculturalism has existed as long as humans have interacted with—either on friendly or feuding terms—other groups of humans. The interesting thing is that the concept has become more magnified today because of our increasing interconnectedness, and we are more aware of "others" than ever.

History is ripe with examples of how groups of people come into contact with one another. Often, these assimilations contain an unequal power structure as with colonization, slavery, feudalism, etc. We have the rises and falls of empires—such as the Mongols, the Ottomans, the Romans, the Mayans, the Tasmanians.

Sometimes, assimilation is a by-product of trade. We have diasporas fueled by trade, based literally on trade winds that dictated the direction of travel for merchants. Trade winds blow east to west just north and south of the equator, consequently influencing the direction ships travel (not to mention storm patterns). One example of this is movement of the Indian Ocean trade routes; today there are Indian communities in New Zealand, Madagascar, Ethiopia that were settled by merchants centuries ago. Let's not forget the Silk Road through China, or the American Railroad.

There are religious repercussions, like the Camino de Santiago and the hajj, Buddha's path. A modern example: In Kevin Kwan's book *Rich People Problems*, one of his characters comments, "if it wasn't for missionaries running amok in China after England won the Opium Wars, we'd all be Buddhists." The fictional family, the Youngs, were the first Christians in southern China, a consequence of the English presence in China in the Opium War period. Who knows when and if Christianity would have reached China if it hadn't been for this European presence.

THE MIND IS JUST LIKE A MUSCLE

In fact, by 1450, 90% of humans lived in a single mega-world of Afro-Asia, which includes most modern-day Asia, Europe, and Africa, as a result of European exploration vis-a-vis trade, exploration, and wealth accumulation.

Despite the interconnectedness of our planet, interconnectedness does not equal homogeneity. While we have a single global "culture" that is divided into internationally recognized states and the same capitalist market forces, human rights, and international law, as well as scientific knowledge, we also maintain distinct identities on many levels (national, state, local, individual) that highlight these differences, these multiple coexisting cultures. Microcultures, if you will.

> Cultures have coexisted and commingled since groups of humans came into contact with one another. What's new is our awareness of how this commingling affects people on a relationship level, on a person-to-person level.

The point is: cultures have coexisted and commingled since groups of humans came into contact with one another. What's new is our awareness of how this commingling affects people on a relationship level, on a person-to-person level.

We've discussed the importance of building awareness around how interconnectedness can affect us on an individual level, and how these effects can in turn create a different set of challenges for society at large, namely prejudice in the form of bias, racism, and stereotypes. It's this awareness that helps us exercise our brains, grow, and become stronger humans and citizens of the world.

Next, we'll look at how the media affects the ways we build awareness of our peers and of ourselves.

MEDIA

In our digital age, dictated by various screen sizes and voices like Alexa and Siri, the evolving nature of media has an immeasurable impact on how we consume information.

Quartz published an article about the ramifications for bias on platforms like TikTok, an app created in China in 2016 that, two years later, surpassed Instagram with the greatest number of downloads.

Research finds content of videos from TikTok often features white teens imitating stereotypical lifestyles or characteristics of black people or other people of color. Examples of this include changing their accents, using slang, and gesturing various mannerisms seemingly in good fun. Some people are sharing these videos as a source of entertainment. Some are intentionally perpetuating racist cliches. That's the reality. That's also an opportunity for education.

These cliches date back to the 1820s, pre-Civil War times when slavery was an integral part of economic subsistance. Blackface, a performance where white actors would paint their faces black, often appeared in minstrel shows that depicted people of African descent in comical forms. Post-Civil War, racial tensions were especially

THE MIND IS JUST LIKE A MUSCLE

pronounced. During these performances, black people were portrayed as lazy, stupid, ignorant, criminal, and hyper-sexual. The legacy of these shows led to blatantly negative stereotypes used in advertising, propaganda, literature, and film. Jim Crow, for whom the Jim Crow laws are named, was one of the first fictional blackface characters on record in pop culture.

Aside: there are many fictional characters that act as tropes, or metaphors, throughout history and literature. These include Prince Charming, Marmy, Rosie the Riveter, and Peter Pan. It's fascinating to think about the people who have influenced our ideas of how society operates or should operate, who never actually *lived*.

Are you aware of how videos depicting these behaviors can be viewed as racism? Maybe you are, maybe you aren't.

What's interesting is, there's so much content available online that serves the purpose of broadening our horizons and educating us on different people and cultures across the world. But there's a catch.

Remember the details about filter bubbles and social media in Part I? If you and another person search for a term at the same moment, the Internet's individualized algorithms can provide different results to each of you. Also, on social media, we tend to follow our friends who have similar beliefs and backgrounds to us—socioeconomic, religious, political, and otherwise.

As a result, many teens today learn about other cultures from the media they're consuming on a regular basis (i.e. YouTube, Instagram, Snapchat, Netflix, and other streaming services), rather than having real-life relationships and friendships with people who belong to the cultures they're ironically viewing online. This is difficult when, as we just noted, our upbringings are influenced quite handily by our immediate communities: our households, schools, and neighborhoods. The consequences of this "real-life" segregation, paired with access to social media, include an unconscious perpetuation of stereotypes.

In a way, it's a chicken-and-egg problem. What comes first—awareness or bias? Based on the research, bias is more natural to us, but our consciousness gives us the benefit of awareness if we're willing to exercise our brains. After all, the brain is just like a muscle. Remember, building awareness is like building muscle—only in our cranium and not on our biceps. It's a strength that will help us in the long run. If we don't maintain it, it will atrophy and go limp.

If people had more control over what they consumed online, would the world be more aware? If we didn't have such curated algorithms, what would we see? What would the first result of a search query be, for you versus for me? We can think of "the web" as an influencer in itself, much like our family, our school, our neighborhood, our circle of friends. The thing is, today it seems we control what gets served to us online as little or as much as we can control who our parents or siblings are.

Getting back to the TikTok example, if I know that there's a negative history associated with some of the content and what it represents, does that make it okay for me to consume or create because I'm aware and don't actively believe in those things, and I'm just doing it for entertainment? I'd argue no, it's not okay, because that is a conscious choice to participate. It's the idea of focusing on what you can control.

So if I wanted to diversify the kind of information I have access to, what can I do? We'll get to that in Part III.

SCHOOLS

Aside from bias across racial lines, what about gender? In 2014, it was leaked that a group of male high school students in Newport Beach, California were hosting a draft for female prom dates. The draft resembled something like how professional sports teams take turns selecting eligible players from a specified pool each season. The principal at the time wrote in a memo to parents that "it is not okay for any student to feel objectified or judged in any way." While I agree with the sentiment, students are being judged everyday—on the basis of their academic performance. They're being ranked and graded and tested across all kinds of "indicators of success".

The difference is, the prom draft is making judgements using criteria that is inconsistent with the values of school administrators. It's a classic example of "what we don't know scares us". Until then, this approach was unfamiliar. Some might describe it as innovative. Some might describe it as objectification. Is the prom draft inherently wrong, morally and ethically? The intent —at its core, to solve a problem—is not malicious. But even so, does that make it okay? What is the school's role? What is the school's responsibility? What is the parent's responsibility? What is the students' responsibility? Where should the boundary be drawn? What is the answer?

In the wake of this story making headlines in national news, the school hired an ethics consultant to provide training for students in diversity, honesty, inclusivity, and ethics. Using such events as an opportunity for education and creating awareness is a good start, for students and administrators alike.

PEOPLE IN POWER

A study conducted by Princeton University found that with time, people can adapt to societal diversity and actually benefit from it. Those in power especially set the tone for integrating people into a new society. Without getting into too much detail, the study focused on religious diversity, which has been well recorded in research as a convenient way to measure social diversity.

In short, researchers found that over short two-year periods, an increase in religious diversity reduced social trust, thus undermining the quality of life. And yet, over a longer twelve-year period, diversity led to greater intergroup contact that increased social trust to offset the negative short-term influence of diversity on quality of life.

So, we can presume that as time passes and as awareness grows and develops, the benefits of diversity outweigh the initial jolts of discomfort/fear/bias that our brains predispose us to feeling. Remember, the brain is just like a muscle and needs to be exercised for optimum use.

These findings have important policy implications, especially for immigration reform. Whenever people feel insecure for economic reasons and society is also changing around them, it becomes tempting for politicians to blame immigrants for these feelings of insecurity when this is not really the case. It is up to political leaders to set the right tone and message to counteract distrust in the short term so as to encourage integration in the long run.

The study's authors suggest that, "If you give people who are different from you half a chance, they will integrate into society pretty well. It is when you purposefully push them out, or erect barriers against them, that problems are introduced...It's important for our political leaders to set the right tone, so proper integration can occur."

TYING IT ALL TOGETHER

Not all cultures (or politics, for that matter) are characterized by the same level of acceptance. Which begs the question, is acceptance cultural? Perhaps acceptance starts on an individual level and becomes cultural, like the use of tools and food production (Jared Diamond takes a deep-dive into this idea in his work titled *Guns, Germs, and Steel*). We need to look both inside and outside the household to understand each other and ourselves.

PART III: TAKING ACTION WITH EXERCISE

We've explored the human brain and read about how the way it's built can influence the way we see and experience the world. There is still much more to be researched, learned, and applied about these topics. We are making progress by pushing forward to uncover and understand what is unknown.

Part III is devoted to actionable steps you can take to give your brain some exercise and help it get better and stronger.

We'll explore some questions you can ask yourself about . . . yourself, and how you currently engage with the world in the Internal Dialogue section.

Next, we'll take a look at the actions we take in our day to day life, make observations about these patterns of behaviors, and see where changes might be beneficial.

THE MIND IS JUST LIKE A MUSCLE

Finally, we'll weave it all together in a step-by-step plan that helps us be accountable for the choices and actions we make, conscious or unconscious, intentional or not.

INTERNAL DIALOGUE

What are some questions you can ask yourself about your own points of view, opinions, thoughts, and musings? It's also important, if not fundamentally critical, to consider the sources you're using as the basis to form your position.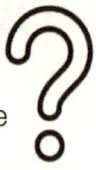

Of course, we all have our beliefs, but reinforcing the importance of education and empathy, it's important to be aware of and accept differing perspectives so that you too can better support your own position. It's also important to consider there are pros and cons to most positions (which is the subject of another book entirely), and just because someone has a different point of view doesn't make them wrong or right. Yes, we can argue there are ideas and concepts that are inherently bad, like mass genocide, rape, etc. But there are also ideas where there is more gray than distinct black and white. It's in the gray where we will have the most conflict, the most disagreement, the most conversation. And, quite frankly, the most discomfort. That's where change happens—at the edge of your comfort zone.

So let's get familiar with discomfort and growth—both of which we experience during exercise, even and especially when we exercise our brains.

QUESTIONS ABOUT:

My Point of View

- How do I react when my viewpoint is challenged?
- How many friends or acquaintances do I have whose views differ from mine?
- Have I considered that I might be wrong about some things? What would that mean? How can I accept that and be better?

Too much too soon? Maybe start with a particular event or belief you have, like who you plan to vote for in an election, or a recent decision your school or employer made.

Current Events or New Information

- What about this information makes me believe it/him/her?
- Is this information from a trustworthy source?
- What percentage of my information comes from this source?
- Have I done my due diligence and researched the subject? Or did I hear it randomly and decide to support it because it's consistent with what I already believe? I.e., do I feel challenged or reinforced by this information?
- Do I have all the information? What's missing?

Now go back to your own internal dialogue and ask yourself . . .

My Point of View

- How do I react when my viewpoint is challenged?
- How many friends or acquaintances do I have whose views differ from mine?

- Have I considered that I might be wrong about some things? What would that mean? How can I accept that and be better?

ACTIONABLE AWARENESS

Next, let's take inventory of how and where you're spending your money, your time, and your energy.

Consider the following:

1. Who do you follow on social media?
2. Where do you get your news?
3. Where do you spend your money?
4. When you see something that you disagree with, do you say something?

Who do you follow on social media?

Open up your apps and audit who you're following. Identify patterns. The most important thing is to ask yourself, in what way is this person similar to me? In what way is this person different from me?

 Follow people who come from different backgrounds than you.

If you're feeling ambitious, see if you can make that number match your current "following" number so you basically double your sources of information. Start with one social media platform first, maybe the one you use the most, and expand from there.

Where do you get your news?

This is similar to the social media question. Think about where you get the bulk of your news. These days, news and media outlets can seem synonymous. Most of the large newspapers and local news stations, for example, have their own Instagram and/or Twitter accounts. Municipalities are adding social media accounts to their bevy of ways to disseminate and share information related to their programs, agendas, and activities. Most people have one or two go-tos for their local, state, national, or international updates. What are some other sources that you might add to your mix? It's not only a question of accuracy (which is obviously important and an indication of responsible journalism) but also of being aware of what others might be hearing.

> **CHALLENGE:** Look up news outlets in your city, county or region. Follow at least two different sources—one newspaper and one municipal source—so you're getting some variety in news. If you're feeling ambitious, look up news outlets across your state, the nation, and the world. You'll be moved by the different approaches to "news" that exist out there.

Where do you spend your money?

An important question that we sometimes forget to ask ourselves. With the likes of big business, including the Amazons, Targets, and Costcos of the world, we forget there are smaller, locally based, independently owned businesses we could support with our dollars in addition to these other retailers. Remember, we live in a capitalistic society, and where we spend our money matters.

> **CHALLENGE:** Keep track of where you're spending for a week or two, or 20-ish transactions. Where are you spending? Big business, small business? Consider what you're buying and how you might be able to shift some of your spending to smaller, locally based, independently owned businesses. (This is also a good exercise to see how and where you spend *in general.* I do this exercise once every three months and it's crazy to see how easy it is to make adjustments if you know where you're starting from.)

When you see something that you disagree with, do you say something?

This is a tricky one. In concept, wouldn't it be great if we literally spoke up every time something bothered us or went against our beliefs? This goes back to the idea of acceptance, that accepting people is critical to our peace. However, there is a gray area where right and wrong commingle from time to time.

We live in a country based on freedoms. I use the plural here because there are many dimensions to the freedoms we have rights to, as outlined in our constitution. However, the ways these freedoms have been enforced over time are anything but equal in execution. It's one of the great inconsistencies of humanity we learned about in Part I. While we consciously believe we are fair and unbiased in our behaviors and actions, we might in fact be unconsciously unfair and full of bias. Also, as we've learned, we have the ability to choose, to inform ourselves and take action when we see inconsistencies playing out in our families, our friend groups, our communities, our businesses, and our country.

CHALLENGE: When you see something you disagree with, take action in a way that suits you. Sometimes, I must point out, it will be necessary to invite some discomfort to the party and live on the edge of your comfort zone. But on a day to day basis, the key is to create sustainable behaviors that allow for sustainable action. I think this IG post sums it up better than my words can:

> some are posting on social media
> some are protesting in the streets
> some are donating silently
> some are educating themselves
> some are having tough conversations with friends & family
>
> a revolution has many lanes — be kind to yourself and to others who are traveling in the same direction
>
> just keep your foot on the gas

Viola Davis (and others) posted these words in wake of the deaths of George Floyd (and Breonna Taylor and Ahmaud Arbery and others) in the spring of 2020. While these words are specific to combatting the systemic racism that permeates the very structures of our corporations and politics, the sentiment rings true when it comes to any and all forms of wrong we witness. And so, to reiterate—take action that suits you, but be consistent and sustain the behavior, because that's the only way change happens.

CONCLUDING WORDS

We've covered a lot of stuff here. We learned about how the brain is its own filter that influences how we see and experience the world. We learned that, as a result of this filter, we develop biases because of how our brains are wired. While we can't control the individual neurons inside our brains that create these biases, we *can* control how we respond to the world around us. We do this by exercising our minds, by making our brains stronger through education and awareness.

The only constant is change. This is true today more than ever. While the world can be overwhelming, stressful, and at times very scary, the most important thing we can do is focus on what we can control. What does that mean for you? Whatever it is, don't let your mind atrophy and sit there, disengaged. The brain is just like a muscle. Make sure it gets the workouts it needs to get stronger.

THANK YOU!

I am so appreciative of you taking the time to read this book. I hope you found value in its content.

If you enjoyed *The Mind Is Just Like A Muscle*, and would be willing to spare just two or three minutes . . . please share your review of the book on my website:

www.bysarasalam.com

Reviews help me get the book into as many hands as possible, and support my work as an author for the long-term (my dream!).

I'm grateful for your support and look forward to sharing more of my work with you!

ACKNOWLEDGMENTS

I wrote this book to bring awareness to how and why the modern world is affecting people, especially teenagers. I chose to focus on teens because these years are crucial for forming ideas about the self and the world. Adults too can benefit from this content, because learning is a life-long process and it's never too late to learn something new.

The Mind Is Just Like A Muscle provides a different perspective on how people are handling living in the most complicated time in human history. Our lives are flashes of light compared to the age of our planet. We feel like living a century is a long period of time, but really it's the blink of an eye in the history of the world. When we take a step back, we can see that time moves us along, though slowly and steadily. The impacts of this are great. The key is that while technology and innovation are evolving on a daily basis, our brains—our de facto filter and most important tool—are not. What does this mean for how we think about the world? Everything.

I'm grateful for the opportunity to share my perspectives on how we can approach living in modern America in a manner that's thoughtful and inquisitive, while also admitting there's so much we're still learning.

I'm grateful for the research being conducted to expand our understanding of what we're grappling with and how to make sense of it. (Special shout out to those who participated in my field research and shared personal histories that helped shape my positions and viewpoints. Thank you!) I'm grateful for challengers to my thinking, who poke holes in my logic and encourage me to revisit my conclusions and make my positions stronger.

And as always, I'm grateful for the support of family and friends who motivate me to keep going.

ABOUT THE AUTHOR

Sara Salam is an award-winning author, editor and poet. Published since age 11, Sara writes nonfiction, fiction, and poetry. Sara uses her experiences as a ten-year Human Resources professional, consultant and journalist to bring awareness to how and why the modern world is affecting people: its indelible impact on humans, the science of it, and how to navigate it. Sara is a proud UCLA Bruin and active in her community of Newport Beach. She enjoys writing, yoga and the beach.

© 2020 Sara Salam

www.bysarasalam.com

@bysarasalam

Sara Salam

APPENDIX: NOTES FROM MY BLOG

CUES FROM CAREER DAY

ORIGINALLY PUBLISHED ON MARCH 26, 2018

www.sarasalam.wordpress.com

This past Friday, I participated in La Granada Elementary's Career Day festivities alongside fifteen other working professionals. There was a pilot, a judge, a pediatrician, a counselor, a firefighter, an entrepreneur. We spoke to children—grades 1st through 5th—about our career paths, educational backgrounds, critical workplace challenges, among other topics.

I cannot express how meaningful it was to speak with the keepers of our future. What's more, is that these future members of our workforce will likely encounter a workplace landscape unlike any we've witnessed to date.

> Mercer anticipates 65% of current primary school children will be in jobs that don't exist today.

The World Economic Forum conducted research that found current leading companies believe skills like complex problem-solving and creativity will be most valued as companies' human capital needs shift and evolve.

What are the implications?

For education, we need to revisit how our educational institutions are set up, and consider a structure that invites opportunities for students to build these skills. Does this require a complete overhaul? Not necessarily. But it does require the foresight to incorporate adaptability that aligns with the dynamic nature of today's and future workplace. This Huffpost article investigates this idea in greater detail: https://www.huffingtonpost.ca/craig-and-marc-kielburger/future-job-market_b_16687862.html

For the current workplace, we need to begin to shift our expectations for our workforce and what they might bring to a job. For mid-level employees and above especially, it's unlikely they will have the "experience" we have based our hiring processes on in recent memory—simply because many newly created jobs have not existed before.

Take a Social Media Director, for example: a very small percentage of the workforce has upwards of 10 years of direct social media experience, as social media has hardly been a primary medium for communication for that long.

This requires a mindset adaptation in how we source and screen for employees. Now, more than ever, it's crucial we consider the whole human—an individual's natural behaviors, skills, habits, and experiences—when evaluating candidacy. *Potential* for success will outweigh *past performance*.

How do we measure candidates for potential? An HBR explores this idea here: https://hbr.org/2014/07/the-future-of-talent-is-potential

Exposing our youth to the professional world will always be important. In fact, I'd argue it should be a requirement that working professionals visit a classroom each year to share their work experiences. There are, however, modifications that should be made—to educational curriculums as well as current hiring practices—especially as we move towards a business environment that has heretofore never existed.

ARE YOU AWARE?

ORIGINALLY PUBLISHED NOVEMBER 21, 2017

www.sarasalam.wordpress.com

Self-awareness and how people consciously acknowledge each other's similarities and differences is not a new idea but has gained traction in response to the complexities upending our workplace.

The most common example we hear of is what Daniel Goleman coined as "Emotional intelligence" (sometimes also called EI or EQ), or the ability to identify and regulate your own feelings, and the feelings of people around you.

In concert with Daniel Goleman, there are individuals out there discussing other types of "intelligence."

Barbara Annis, for example, coined the term "Gender Intelligence" in the early 1990s. Her company "recognizes, values, and leverages" gender differences to drive results.
(See http://www.genderintelligence.com/)

In addition, Harvard Business Review published an article by P. Christopher Earley and Elaine Mosakowski in October 2004 about "Cultural Intelligence," or "an outsider's seemingly natural ability to interpret someone's unfamiliar and ambiguous gestures the way that person's compatriots would." (See https://hbr.org/2004/10/cultural-intelligence)

Each of these frameworks seeks to demonstrate value in the conscious effort of understanding your peers from a particular vantage point i.e. emotional, gender, cultural.

Regardless of which approach resonates with you, the key takeaway is self-awareness and being intentional and thoughtful in your approach is critical to your success in today's chaotic landscape of a workplace.

THE HR LADY

ORIGINALLY PUBLISHED AUGUST 10, 2017

www.sarasalam.wordpress.com

WHO SHE IS

I believe happiness is a choice. I smile often and address people by name as much as I can. "So cute, so fun," is my personal slogan. I can't sit at my desk for more than 25 minutes before I physically crave facetime (not the app) with another human. I probably cuss 20 times a day. I thoroughly enjoy puns, especially when it comes to nail polish colors.

I'm also known as "The HR Lady."

An HR professional for the better part of 5 years, I've built my professional brand around my ability to connect with and relate to people. Just south of 30 years old, and therefore a member of the millennial generation, three words my colleagues would use to describe me are happy, fun, and approachable.

*As an aside—The evolution of the HR field is a different topic for a different time, but truth be told the internal tension within the field itself—which advocates both on behalf of the employer and the employee—is a slippery slope in its simplest form and has implications at every level at every company. (Again, for another time.)

The first time one of my colleagues referred to me as The HR Lady I didn't think anything of it. The more frequent the mention this label became, the more it caused me to spend time exploring its origin— why, I, Sara Salam, had become affiliated with this persona.

WHAT SHE SEES

Obvious answer: I work in "HR" and am, on most days, a hard-working businesswoman. Humans tend to defer to familiar categories, in the form of stereotypes and other frames of reference to make sense of our world as we navigate our everyday lives. If we didn't, we wouldn't be able to attempt to process, let alone understand, the now 11 million bits of stimuli (it's true!) coming our way at any given moment.

This protection mechanism initially developed as a way for early humans to quickly distinguish between friends and enemies. Even with this biological shortcut, we're still at a disadvantage given the changing landscape brought about by the Information Age. Our grandparents saw as many people in one month as we do in one day. Our innate biology struggles to keep up with this avalanche of data, which is a recent development as of the past 20 years, which is a conservative estimate of time.

The challenge is that oftentimes, in light of our biology, we miss out on the whole story. We neglect what might be crucial pieces of information that could shed light on untouched parts of the narrative, and therefore end up with a completely different story entirely. Each individual has their own filter through which they experience the world, which is both a benefit and a challenge that we will explore shortly.

This unconscious bias is human. What also makes us human are our biological needs—be they physical, emotional, mental, or spiritual. A New York Times article, Why We Hate Work, explains:

> Employees are vastly more satisfied and productive, it turns out, when four of their core needs are met: physical, through opportunities to regularly renew and recharge at work; emotional, by feeling valued and appreciated for their contributions; mental, when they have the opportunity to focus in an absorbed way on their most important tasks and define when and where they get their work done; and spiritual, by doing more of what they do best and enjoy most, and by feeling connected to a higher purpose at work.

While every human has these core needs, every human by nature is unique. Again, we each have our own filter through which we experience the world, colored by our parents, our hometowns, travels, relationships, etc. Everyone has a different story, different strengths, different things that make us great. Nike rolled out a campaign in 2012 called "Find Your Greatness." It highlights exactly this – that everyone is different, and everyone can be great. It's about identifying what that greatness is and creating your value around it.

Too often, in the hustle of our corporate day-to-day, we forget it is human beings that are running our companies. As Thomas Stewart describes in Intellectual Capital, "the most essentially human tasks:

sensing, judging, creating, and building relationships" are now the most valuable aspects of jobs. It's therefore the thoughts, feelings, and choices generated by the human mind that determine how valuable a company could be. It's crucial we as employers understand our people, including what they're thinking, why they're thinking it, and the behaviors we see as a result. Only then can we take appropriate action to build a workplace attractive, compelling, and motivating to our people, so we can put them in a position to do their best work.

Consider this: if people didn't worry about threats to their core needs (i.e. mental, physical, emotional, spiritual), how much more time and effort could they allocate towards focusing on moving the company towards achieving its goals?

To complicate matters, we now have infinite tools, brought about by what could be argued as the next technological revolution, that have led to an accelerated pace at which work is performed, and with it higher expectations by employers to get work done. Acceleration of productivity is one thing, but if you're accelerating without regard for informed, human choices and thoughtful reassessment as needed, you increase the opportunity for misplaced momentum in the wrong direction, whatever that might mean for your business. It then becomes more difficult to keep your people onboard with your vision, should you need to reset and change course too many times. Confidence is lost. Trust is compromised. People revert back to spending time thinking about their own security/core needs, instead of focusing on making their jobs more valuable.

HOW SHE WORKS

I view my role as a partner to our business: how can we put our **people** in the best position to succeed in their own jobs, in the most effective and efficient way, so that they can dedicate their efforts delivering for the business and not focused on basic human necessities. Traditional "benefits", in the form of medical, dental, and vision coverage, and retirement have historically addressed this idea. Today, in this networked and info-saturated era, these human needs have come to transcend the personal and professional boundary, and as these boundaries becomes less finite, a refresh in philosophy becomes pivotal to the success of business and the engagement of their people.

Humans are social animals, and while some humans are more social than others, there still exists an underlying need for community and sense of belonging. That does not stop in the workplace (which is it's own community) especially as work/life integration, as compared to work/life balance, becomes the standard. These "benefits" now extend to include "life hacks" such as daily meals, fitness reimbursements, staff happy hours and the like.

Therefore, my day-to-day consists of asking lots of questions, asking our people what they want their outcome to be, what tools do they have that can help them get there, what support they need outside of their own resources. Then we figure out how to help them make it happen. People are SO smart; when prompted with the right questions, it's amazing what they'll accomplish with what they already have, or not much else.

It's a uniquely and distinctly human act that the HR Lady would develop an identity in the workplace as such. Oftentimes I'm the defacto-benefits expert, internal therapist, brand ambassador, compliance officer, salesperson and cheerleader. Because that, on the surface, is the role I play and the persona I embody, given the perspective (Humans are awesome!) with which I approach my role.

In acknowledging we are all human, and every human's nature is different, we can foster an environment that breeds success, whatever that means for each person in their role at their organization. It's up to our leaders to identify what these are, and leverage them in each of their people, to optimize not only job performance but engagement and sense of purpose.

Remember, we are all human. All humans are different by nature. In these differences lie our greatness. Find your greatness. Remember YOU are human. Repeat.

Don't forget that I, the HR Lady, too, am human.

REFERENCES

INTRODUCTION

Flynn, R. (2018, December 4). Is The Brain A Muscle? The Truth About The Brain. Retrieved September 9, 2020, from https://blog.mindvalley.com/is-the-brain-a-muscle/

Hoffman, W. (2016, July 29). Bioscience will accelerate East-West convergence in the century ahead. Retrieved January 27, 2020, from https://www.brookings.edu/blog/techtank/2015/07/30/bioscience-will-accelerate-east-west-convergence-in-the-century-ahead/

Hoomans, D. (n.d.). 35,000 Decisions: The Great Choices of Strategic Leaders. Retrieved January 27, 2020, from https://go.roberts.edu/leadingedge/the-great-choices-of-strategic-leaders

Leonard, J. (2020, January 8). Building muscle with exercise: How muscle builds, routines, and diet. Retrieved January 27, 2020, from https://www.medicalnewstoday.com/articles/319151

Lesson 1: Economic Growth and Scarcity. Foundation For Teaching Economics. Retrieved September 30, 2020, from https://www.fte.org/teachers/teacher-resources/lesson-plans/efllessons/lesson-1-economic-growth-and-scarcity/

Managing Unconscious Bias. (2017, March). Speech presented at LA Clippers Unconscious Bias Staff Training in CA, Los Angeles.

Mier, T. (2020, September 8). After her death, a debate about gender identity. *Los Angeles Times*, p. B1.

Regalado, A. (2020, June 18). More than 26 million people have taken an at-home ancestry test. Retrieved August 27, 2020, from https://www.technologyreview.com/2019/02/11/103446/more-than-26-million-people-have-taken-an-at-home-ancestry-test/

Rollins, H. (n.d.). ARE YOU AN EXTROVERT, INTROVERT, OR AMBIVERT? Retrieved January 27, 2020, from https://www.themuseatdreyfoos.com/top-stories/2018/02/21/are-you-an-extrovert-introvert-or-ambivert/

Understanding the Butterfly Effect. (2017, June 12). Retrieved August 27, 2020, from https://www.americanscientist.org/article/understanding-the-butterfly-effect

PART I

Beauman, J., Alberts, N., Simmons, A., Connolly, M., & Ellin, A. (n.d.). Psychological Projection: Dealing With Undesirable Emotions: Everyday Health. Retrieved February 4, 2020, from https://www.everydayhealth.com/emotional-health/psychological-projection-dealing-with-undesirable-emotions/

Carr, N. G. (2010). *The shallows: What the Internet is doing to our brains*. New York: W.W. Norton.

Causey, K., & Goetz, A. (2009, July 02). The Halo Effect in Overdrive. Retrieved February 6, 2020, from https://www.psychologytoday.com/us/blog/natural-history-the-modern-mind/200907/the-halo-effect-in-overdrive

Cherry, K. (2020, February 19). Why Do We Favor Information That Confirms Our Existing Beliefs? Retrieved August 27, 2020, from https://www.verywellmind.com/what-is-a-confirmation-bias-2795024

Color Blindness. (n.d.). Retrieved August 28, 2020, from https://www.nei.nih.gov/learn-about-eye-health/eye-conditions-and-diseases/color-blindness

Dell Technologies. (2018). *Realizing 2030: A Divided Vision of the Future* (Rep.). London, UK: Vanson Bourne. Retrieved August 28, 2020, from https://www.delltechnologies.com/content/dam/delltechnologies/assets/perspectives/2030/pdf/Realizing-2030-A-Divided-Vision-of-the-Future-Summary.pdf.

Depalma, A. (1995, June 11). The World; Racism? Mexico's in Denial. *New York Times*. Retrieved February 4, 2020, from https://www.nytimes.com/1995/06/11/weekinreview/the-world-racism-mexico-s-in-denial.html

Diene, D. (2006). *RACISM, RACIAL DISCRIMINATION, XENOPHOBIA AND ALL FORMS OF DISCRIMINATION Report of the Special Rapporteur on contemporary forms of racism, racial discrimination, xenophobia and related intolerance, Addendum* MISSION TO JAPAN* (Rep.). New York, NY: United Nations Economic and Social Council. doi:https://web.archive.org/web/20061214115324/http://imadr.org/geneva/2006/G0610396.pdf

Erickson, T. (2014, August 23). How Mobile Technologies Are Shaping a New Generation. Retrieved August 27, 2020, from https://hbr.org/2012/04/the-mobile-re-generation

Experts, K. (Ed.). (n.d.). Brain and Nervous System (for Parents) - Nemours KidsHealth. Retrieved February 4, 2020, from https://kidshealth.org/en/parents/brain-nervous-system.html

Harari, Y. N. (2019). *21 lessons for the 21st century*. London: Vintage.

Harari, Y. N., Purcell, J., & Watzman, H. (2018). *Sapiens: A brief history of humankind*. New York, NY: Harper Perennial.

How to Reduce Unconscious Bias in the Workplace. (2020, August 14). Retrieved August 27, 2020, from https://lattice.com/library/how-to-reduce-unconscious-bias-at-work

Izecksohn, V. (2006). Race, State, and Armed Forces in Independence-Era Brazil: Bahia, 1790s-1840s. *Hispanic American Historical Review, 86*(1), 176-178. doi:10.1215/00182168-86-1-176

Juliana Menasce Horowitz, A. (2020, August 20). Views on Race in America 2019. Retrieved January 31, 2020, from https://www.pewsocialtrends.org/2019/04/09/race-in-america-2019/

Mcleod, S. (n.d.). Solomon Asch - Conformity Experiment. Retrieved January 29, 2020, from https://www.simplypsychology.org/asch-conformity.html

Menzies, G. (2002). *1421: The year that China discovered the world*. London: Bantam Press.

Patel, H. (1972). General Amin and the Indian Exodus from Uganda. *Issue: A Journal of Opinion, 2*(4), 12-22. doi:10.2307/1166488

Penn, J. (Host). (2019, October 13). *The Creative Penn* [Podcast]. Retrieved February 3, 2020, from How to write a novel in a month #nanowrimo with Grant Faulkner

Unconscious Bias. (n.d.). Retrieved August 27, 2020, from https://diversity.ucsf.edu/resources/unconscious-bias

University of California - Riverside. (2019, July 8). 'You all look alike to me' is hard-wired in us, research finds: Less differentiation in other-race facial features occurs in the earliest cognitive processes. *ScienceDaily*. Retrieved March 1, 2020 from www.sciencedaily.com/releases/2019/07/190708112419.htm

University of Cambridge. (2020, January 29). Brain networks come 'online' during adolescence to prepare teenagers for adult life. *ScienceDaily*. Retrieved August 27, 2020 from www.sciencedaily.com/releases/2020/01/200129104705.htm

U.S. population by generation 2019. (2020, July 20). Retrieved August 27, 2020, from https://www.statista.com/statistics/797321/us-population-by-generation/

Waugh, R. (2017, May 04). This map shows the most racist countries in Europe (and how Britain ranks). Retrieved March 1, 2020, from https://metro.co.uk/2017/05/03/this-map-shows-the-most-racist-countries-in-europe-and-how-britain-ranks-6612608/

What is a Filter Bubble? - Definition from Techopedia. (n.d.). Retrieved August 27, 2020, from https://www.techopedia.com/definition/28556/filter-bubble

Xenophobia. (2020, August 03). Retrieved August 27, 2020, from https://en.wikipedia.org/wiki/Xenophobia

PART II

Brabeck, K. (2017, September 26). Beyond the "Melting Pot": Why We Need to Support the Multicultural Identities of All America's Children. Retrieved January 15, 2020, from https://psychologybenefits.org/2017/08/29/we-need-to-support-the-multicultural-identities-of-all-americas-children/

Brooks, D. (2020, March 19). The Nuclear Family Was a Mistake. *The Atlantic*. Retrieved April 18, 2020, from https://www.theatlantic.com/magazine/archive/2020/03/the-nuclear-family-was-a-mistake/605536/

Budiman, A. (2020, August 20). Key findings about U.S. immigrants. Retrieved August 27, 2020, from https://www.pewresearch.org/fact-tank/2020/08/20/key-findings-about-u-s-immigrants/

Connor, P., & López, G. (2020, May 30). 5 facts about the U.S. rank in worldwide migration. Retrieved August 27, 2020, from https://www.pewresearch.org/fact-tank/2016/05/18/5-facts-about-the-u-s-rank-in-worldwide-migration/

Elli P. Schachter and Jonathan J. Ventura. Identity Agents: Parents as Active and Reflective Participants in Their Children's Identity Formation. *Journal of Research on Adolescence*, 2008; 18 (3): 449 DOI: 10.1111/j.1532-7795.2008.00567.x

FECYT - Spanish Foundation for Science and Technology. (2009, October 19). Non-nuclear Families Function, Too. *ScienceDaily*. Retrieved January 31, 2020 from www.sciencedaily.com/releases/2009/10/091019123001.htm

Fry, Hannah. CdM High: How the 'prom draft' works. (2014, May 08). *Los Angeles Times*. Retrieved August 27, 2020, from https://www.latimes.com/socal/daily-pilot/news/tn-dpt-me-prom-draft-cdm-boys-venue-20140507-story.html

Fry, Hannah. District hires ethics consultant in wake of cheating scandal. (2014, June 10.) *Los Angeles Times*. Retrieved September 14, 2020, from https://www.latimes.com/socal/daily-pilot/news/tn-dpt-me-0611-ethics-consultant-20140610-story.html

Holt, B. (2019, November 04). Teens on TikTok have no clue they're perpetuating racist stereotypes. *Quartz*. Retrieved February 1, 2020, from https://qz.com/quartzy/1738478/how-teens-on-tiktok-are-perpetuating-racist-stereotypes

I'm sorry that my dog is awesome and behaves better than your children.: Dog quotes, Dog mom, Crazy dog lady. (n.d.). Retrieved August 27, 2020, from https://www.pinterest.de/pin/66357794489026104/

Jean Christophe Meunier, Michael Boyle, Thomas G. O'Connor, Jennifer M. Jenkins. Multilevel Mediation: Cumulative Contextual Risk, Maternal Differential Treatment, and Children's Behavior Within Families. *Child Development*, 2013; DOI: 10.1111/cdev.12066

Kim, J. S. (2014). *Solution-focused brief therapy: A multicultural approach.* Los Angeles, CA: SAGE.

Kristin L. Moilanen, Mary Lynn Manuel. Helicopter Parenting and Adjustment Outcomes in Young Adulthood: A Consideration of the Mediating Roles of Mastery and Self-Regulation. *Journal of Child and Family Studies*, 2019; 28 (8): 2145 DOI: 10.1007/s10826-019-01433-5

Lazar, A., Karlan, D., & Salter, J. (2011). *The 101 most influential people who never lived: How characters of fiction, myth, legends, television, and movies have shaped our society, changed our behavior, and set the course of history.* New York, NY: Bristol Park Books.

Leins, C. (2019, December 19). These Are the 5 Youngest Countries in the World. Retrieved August 27, 2020, from https://www.usnews.com/news/best-countries/slideshows/these-are-the-5-youngest-countries-in-the-world

Livingston, G. (2020, May 30). The rise of multiracial and multiethnic babies in the U.S. Retrieved August 27, 2020, from https://www.pewresearch.org/fact-tank/2017/06/06/the-rise-of-multiracial-and-multiethnic-babies-in-the-u-s/

Lopez, M., Krogstad, J., & Passel, J. (2020, August 18). Who is Hispanic? Retrieved August 27, 2020, from https://www.pewresearch.org/fact-tank/2019/11/11/who-is-hispanic/

Miguel R. Ramos, Matthew R. Bennett, Douglas S. Massey, Miles Hewstone. Humans adapt to social diversity over time. *Proceedings of the National Academy of Sciences*, 2019; 201818884 DOI: 10.1073/pnas.1818884116

Ming-Te Wang, Sarah Kenny. Longitudinal Links Between Fathers' and Mothers' Harsh Verbal Discipline and Adolescents' Conduct Problems and Depressive Symptoms. *Child Development*, 2013; DOI: 10.1111/cdev.12143

Roberto Baiocco, Nicola Carone, Salvatore Ioverno, Vittorio Lingiardi. Same-Sex and Different-Sex Parent Families in Italy. *Journal of Developmental & Behavioral Pediatrics*, 2018; DOI: 10.1097/DBP.0000000000000583

Sarah R. Brauner-Otto, William G. Axinn, Dirgha J. Ghimire. Parents' Marital Quality and Children's Transition to Adulthood. *Demography*, 2020; DOI: 10.1007/s13524-019-00851-w

Sharon Dekel, Barry A. Farber. Models of Intimacy of Securely and Avoidantly Attached Young Adults. *The Journal of Nervous and Mental Disease*, 2012; 200 (2): 156 DOI: 10.1097/NMD.0b013e3182439702

Smith, E. (2016, May 20). Monogamy Is Not "Natural" For Human Beings. Retrieved August 27, 2020, from https://www.psychologytoday.com/us/blog/not-born-yesterday/201605/monogamy-is-not-natural-human-beings

Society for Personality and Social Psychology. (2014, February 13). Understanding everything from family structure to trauma: New technology is yielding bigger data. *ScienceDaily*. Retrieved February 1, 2020 from www.sciencedaily.com/releases/2014/02/140213142315.htm

St John's College, University of Cambridge. (2017, October 5). Prehistoric humans are likely to have formed mating networks to avoid inbreeding. *ScienceDaily*. Retrieved February 4, 2020 from www.sciencedaily.com/releases/2017/10/171005141759.htm

University of Cincinnati. (2008, August 5). The School Bully: Does It Run In The Family?. *ScienceDaily*. Retrieved February 4, 2020 from www.sciencedaily.com/releases/2008/08/080804111636.htm

University of Illinois at Urbana-Champaign. (2010, February 22). Are Latino teens sexual risk takers? It's complicated, researcher says. *ScienceDaily*.

Retrieved February 3, 2020 from www.sciencedaily.com/releases/2010/02/100222121628.htm

Walker, R. S. (2011). Co-residence patterns in hunter-gatherer societies show unique human social structure. Retrieved February 1, 2020, from https://www.researchgate.net/publication/279286429_Co-residence_patterns_in_hunter-gatherer_societies_show_unique_human_social_structure

PART III

Davis, V. (2020, June 3). Retrieved from www.instagram.com/violadavis

www.ingramcontent.com/pod-product-compliance
Lightning Source LLC
Chambersburg PA
CBHW060402080526
44583CB00012B/442